MARIETTA HOLLEY

Truly yours
Marietta Holley

MARIETTA HOLLEY

Life with "Josiah Allen's Wife"

KATE H. WINTER

SYRACUSE UNIVERSITY PRESS

Syracuse, New York 13244–5160

First Paperback Edition 2005

05 06 07 08 09 10   6 5 4 3 2 1

The paper used in this publication meets the minimum requirements of American National Standard for Information Sciences—Permanence of Paper for Printed Library Materials, ANSI Z39.48–1984∞™

Co-winner of the 1984 John Ben Snow Manuscript Prize.

ISBN 0–8156–3088–3 (pbk.: alk. paper)

Library of Congress Cataloging-in-Publication Data

Winter, Kate H.

Marietta Holley : life with "Josiah Allen's wife."

(A New York State study)

Bibliography: p.

Includes index.

1. Holley, Marietta, 1836–1926. 2. Humorists, American—19th century—Biography. 3. Authors, American—19th century—Biography. 4. New York (State)—Biography. 5. New York (State) in literature. 6. Women in literature. 7. Feminism and literature. I. Title. II. Series.

PS1949.H5Z94   1984   813'4[B]   84–16191

ISBN 0–8156–2324–0

Manufactured in the United States of America

For
GENE,
my own lawful pardner, who never once asked,
"Who will read the book, Samantha,
when it is rote?"

KATE H. WINTER is a lecturer in the English Department at the State University of New York at Albany and is the author of several books, including *Woman in the Mountain: Reconstructions of Self and Land by Adirondack Women Writers.* In 2004, she and WPBS developed a documentary version of *Marietta Holley,* producing the film *Josiah Allen's Wife: The Marietta Holley Story* and winning two awards for excellence in writing, editing, and videography.

CONTENTS

ILLUSTRATIONS

PREFACE TO THE PAPERBACK EDITION

Which is to be read, bein' different from the first but not any better nor any worse.

In the twenty years since this book first appeared, America has been transformed by dynamic and dramatic events—terrorism in the homeland, war abroad, technological and environmental extremes. New York State's "North Country" has not been spared. Dragged into the twenty-first century, the region seems to be in the upswing of its cycle of famine and plenty. The community college is thriving. Village schools have merged into regional high schools embracing neighboring towns and erasing old rivalries. Family farms are inherited and run by young women. Other farms are pieced together into agricultural factories. Patchwork pastures become residential subdivisions. The military "camp," now Fort Drum, has become home to soldiers and families from all over the country who share one commitment: patriotic duty. War is never far from North Country consciousness. When globalization rather than regionalism and rapid change rather than stability are the rule, what does Holley—or Samantha—bring to readers? Enduring, deeply rooted values that sustained Holley, her kin, and her characters: the dignity of work, the simple yardstick of "country" values, regional pride, perseverance against adversity, individual independence, and thoughtful patriotism—the roses hidden under the North Country snow.

In these intervening decades, the discipline of literary studies has changed in some substantial ways, and years of academic neglect of Holley's writing have been redressed. Thanks to the last twenty-five years of research in women's writing and the legitimization of feminist readings, "domestic" concerns and writers concentrating on them are no longer trivialized. In the 1980s, the primary feminist project was to recover Holley's life and work. Since then, the task has been to explore the landscape of her life and writing. The terrain of women's humor—characterized by Nancy Walker as an area of shared comic strategies used by women to critique American culture—has been mapped and mined to explore how humor by women works, and Holley's Samantha has taken her place within that region of laughter. Emily Toth makes clear a context, a lineage, even a tradition of women who deliberately wrote humor rather than simply using humor as one of many literary techniques. Although such new directions in literary criticism as Marxist and materialist critiques have not especially enriched the reading of Holley's life or work, they have focused more attention on the differences—and similarities—between Holley's humor and that of Twain. In *Necessary Madness,* Gregg Camfield's thoughtful discussion of the "work" of domestic humor, the author gives an example of this application of theory and close reading that enlarges our understanding of the writing of both authors.

Twenty years ago, in a corner at a scholarly conference after the panel was finished, someone would quietly ask me if I thought Holley was a lesbian. In her own time, questions about her unmarried state framed her autobiographical representation of herself—Was she unattractive? Unappealing? Odd-looking? Sexually repressed? Afraid of men? Was she vigorous and healthy? What choices did she really have? What sort of spinster was she? Dour? Rigid? A twiggy old maid or a bright, productive solitary? And can a woman be both attractive and funny? It is clear why suffragists Anthony and Stanton implored Holley to kill off Josiah—a widow had more clout than a matron did, and a spinster none at all. In her own time, as well as in the late twentieth century, a widow had her own stamp of validity and approval, a social niche that prevented her sexuality and attractiveness (unlike her bank balance) from automatically coming into question. Even the suggestion that Holley might have had an inappropriate relationship with Lew Hoxie reflects a dominant view of sexual orientation that limited the inquiry into the writer's life. Queer theory has given us permission to ask the questions out loud during the discussion: Did her intense friendships with a few women mask a sexual secret? Were accounts of her marriage proposals and courtships, as well as her choice of "writer" rather than "wife" as a career, excuses to cover a woman-loving sexuality? Perhaps a recently emerging category of sexual orientation that theorists and scientists have begun to explore accounts for difference such as Holley's: Might she best be described as "asexual," something our culture is only now coming to understand as a variety of "normal"?

Not only does queer theory give questions about Holley's private life a vocabulary and legitimacy, but it also demonstrates that the asking is a useful critical strategy. Judith Fetterley and Marjorie Pryse practice invaluable techniques for understanding nineteenth-century women's fiction in *Writing Out Of Place.* Their readings create a context within which the term *queer* refers not just to sexual orientation, to lesbian and gay, but to difference. Like the regionalists Fetterley and Pryse re-read, Holley resists plot, foregrounding characters who are, ironically, not participating in the stories' heterosexual marriage plots, who resist the norm while seeming to conform to it, introducing what is odd, atypical, "queer," different from the national norm—regional. In her own life, Holley's positioning of herself as the head of her household, her insistence on individual freedom in speech, politics, and religious practices, even her domestic arrangements, are richer when read through the prism of the "queer eye." Like Samantha, who strives (though sometimes weakly) for empathy and moderation, queer consciousness opens twenty-first-century readers to broader understandings of "normal, "national," and "different." That may be Holley's greatest value to contemporary readers: empathy. In an age of global rather than regional culture, where terrorism permeates all boundaries, borders, and bodies, finding the empathy to negotiate life in this universe just might be what saves us from ourselves.

Fans of Holley's Samantha stories know that her humor is sometimes self-righteous and heavy-handed, not always maintaining the ideal "megumness" (mediumness or moderation), but to twenty-first-century eyes that may seem appropriate as industrialized, "civilized" cultures continue to exploit the world's women, children, and poor. Critiquing patriarchal thinking is risky business—women's comedy often is not funny to men—but Holley's humor was (and remains) comic to all. We may hear Samantha's voice echoed in the housewife humor of Erma Bombeck, as she expresses the frustrations of domestic life after the vote, two world wars, and the feminist movement. It is enough to make us question how far we have really come. The collective energy of female gatherings—comedy clubs, quilting circles, church choirs, women's auxiliary organizations—creates a safe space for anti-male laughter, but Samantha's work is more solitary as she engages in one-on-one confrontations and debates with Josiah and Betsey, with shopkeepers and politicians, with social movers and shakers. Actress and academic Jane Curry recasts this habit into hilarious monologues in her one-woman show for contemporary audiences, "Samantha 'Rastles' the Woman Question," proving that the issues Holley raises and her approach to them still generate self-conscious laughter in audiences of both "sects."

As I review the list of thanks in the original "Preface" to this book, I am reminded of the good friends, colleagues, and family members who have been with me on this journey. Some of them are gone but never absent. I am especially grateful to Elaine Handley, to my mother, Margaret Hughs, and to my son Jeffrey for enduring love and support. New friends have appeared whom I cherish for their insights and talents: Melanie Smith Golding, who first conceived of the idea for a film of Holley's life; Dr. Greg Gardner, whose commitment and finesse made the Holley project possible; and Tracy Duflo and the crew at WPBS Watertown who made it happen. The list of credits at the close of the resultant film, the award-winning WPBS documentary *Josiah Allen's Wife: The Marietta Holley Story* (2005), includes the creatives who gave so much to that project; I feel honored to know them and to have worked with them.

"Snow and Roses" was the informing motif and working title of the original manuscript of this book. It is also the image that closes the WPBS documentary on Holley. Her ambivalences, and the creative solutions she found to manage them, are embedded in her habit of growing Christmas roses, hellebore, that blossomed in the short days of December. She would brush the snow off them to reveal their glory against the whiteness of a North Country winter. The resilience and resurrection in the image suit the story this biography and the film seek to tell. That there even is such a film is testament to the powerful appeal of her life's narrative. The grassroots movement to have Holley named to the National Women's Hall of Fame is further evidence that her stories—both private and public—continue to interest readers. What does Holley offer us? A window on a world that is mostly lost in homogenized mall culture; a recollection of our differences, roots, and sources of identity; a reminder that the struggles have been long and remain finished, that equity and justice are still contested, that there is still much to be done; and an awareness that our differences and contradictions require creativity and empathy from us as they did from Marietta Holley herself.

PREFACE

WHILE I SORTED THROUGH the materials trying to understand the forces that shaped Marietta Holley's days and work, I found peculiar similarities and coincidences, ways in which the region, history, family, and character affected both our lives and writing. What follows is her story. It is not the life I wished for her or the one local legend created. If there is any fiction or autobiography here, it is unintended and incidental. Nevertheless, as Samantha said in *Samantha at the Centennial:*

> Writers may try to do the very best they can; their minds may be well stabled, and their principles foundered on a rock; their motives as sound as brass, and soarin' and high-toned as anything can be, and still at the same time, they may have a realizin' sense that in spite of all their pains, there is faults in the book.

For all errors in judgment or skill, I accept the responsibility.

For the good things in this book I have many to thank. I am grateful to a scattered group of librarians, archivists, and historians who ferreted out volumes, manuscripts, and photographs. Special thanks go to Bonnie Ross at the Flower Memorial Library in Watertown, New York, and to Laura Scharer at the Jefferson County Historical Society, as well as to the staff at the State University of New York at Albany Interlibrary Loan. I especially thank the librarians in the Special Collection Section of the College Library, State University College at Geneseo, New York, for permission to refer to and quote from Marietta Holley's letter of 8 April 1904 to Mrs. Eaton and the Allyn Kellogg Ford Collection at the Minnesota Historical Society. For her meticulous and patient handling of the manuscript, my sincere thanks to Norah Davis. For other dimensions of the work, my acknowledgments begin with all my family, especially my grandfather and father, who told me the stories that excited my interest and taught me how to tell them myself; my mother, who shared my enthusiasm, the grinding work of research, and the excitement of discovery; and my son Jeffrey, who gave me his encouragement and understanding. I owe a special debt to the people of the North Country who shared their memories, impressions, and time with me. One consequence of my research among them is a renewed appreciation for their kindness and sincerity. The writer is deeply indebted to John B. Johnson, editor and publisher of the *Watertown Daily Times*, for permitting access to newspaper files over a fifteen-year period, the voluminous correspondence of Holley and the late Harold B. Johnson, and his speech at the dedication of the Holley home, 13 July 1947. The members of the South Jefferson County Historical Society were helpful and supportive. My friends Anita and Henry Colby, who first suggested this undertaking, were equally encouraging in many ways.

I am grateful particularly to the women and men who went before me looking hard at women writers and their works. My debt to them is acknowledged in the sources. Facile expressions of gratitude are inadequate to thank John C. Gerber and Rudolf Nelson for their scrupulous chapter-by-chapter readings of the early version of this study. Finally I thank Perry D. Westbrook for writing his own careful studies of nineteenth-century women writers and piloting me through this biographical work.

There is one for whom no thanks are adequate. To him this work is dedicated.

Schenectady, New York KHW
Spring 1984

PROLOGUE

Which is to be read, if it hain't askin' too much of the kind hearted reader.

—Marietta Holley, *My Opinions And Betsey Bobbet's*

SHE WAS CALLED the Female Mark Twain in the popular press, and it was claimed that she had as large an audience as Twain's. From 1873 to 1914 Marietta Holley was one of America's most popular writers, creating one of its most endearing characters—Samantha—and making "Josiah Allen's Wife" a household phrase. In twenty-one books and uncounted short stories, Samantha regaled the country with her "episodin' and allegorin'" in works dealing with the issues personal and political that occupied the thinkers of the age. In fact, during the early years of her literary career, there were many who simply did not believe that Josiah Allen's Wife was a woman at all because the humor, satire, and political arguments were so vigorous and shrewd.

Her works are squarely in the tradition of the male literary comedians—Mark Twain, Josh Billings, Bill Arp, Artemus Ward, and Petroleum V. Nasby. Stylistically Holley depended for much of her humor on the upcountry dialect and the proverbs and maxims mixed with extravagant images that were the stuff of the "crackerbox philosophers." In using cacography and peculiar orthography, she was actually attempting a phonetic transcription of New York State's North Country speech, and in this she was fairly consistent and systematic, unlike Artemus Ward and Josh Billings. Furthermore, Samantha has certain characteristic phrases that she repeats frequently, habits of speech that make her a rounded character, things like "anon or oftener," "to resoom," "episodin' and allegorin'," and "foremothers."

Holley's character used humor for a new end—propaganda for the feminist movement, which had previously been the butt of much comedy. Using the same character types—the wise sage, the foolish foil, the love-starved spinster—she reverses the reader's sympathies to undermine the conventions of the culture regarding the respective roles of men and women. Whereas other comedians had made the woman, particularly the woman's rights advocate, a laughingstock, Holley created a cast of lesser characters who exemplified the absurdities of intemperance and antisuffrage while she maintained the stalwart central character of Samantha as a right-minded, simple country woman whose habits of speech might have been laughable but whose habits of thought were sound and serious. In a further twist, Samantha satirizes women as well as men, thereby winning her male readers with her fair-mindedness as well as her patience and sympathy for her husband, the foolish Josiah.

The earlier women humorists Ann Stephens and Frances Whitcher had primarily concerned themselves with the impact of genteel values on American women, calling attention to the injustices, abuses, and indignities that the tradition of gentility imposes on women. Ann Stephens, the first American woman humorist to write in the vernacular, chose a male naive narrator, Jonathan Slick, for her 1843 work *High Life in New York*, and employed the same epistolary mode that Seba Smith had used.[1] Whitcher, using the dramatic monologue, created a female comic figure in Widow Bedott. It remained for Holley to create a sympathetic comic woman, and she did so even as the peak of interest in dialect humor was being passed.

Holley was one of the first published fiction writers to emerge out of the North Country region of New York State. Her precursor, Frances Whitcher, was from the upstate village of Whitesboro, near Utica. Two years younger than Holley, Whitcher had enjoyed the advantages of town life over farm life and had thus begun publishing earlier. *The Widow Bedott Papers*, published in book form in 1855, created the first feminine comic figure to be portrayed at length, the widow who satirized an eastern small town's genteel society.

But Widow Bedott is not a sympathetic character at all, and she follows in the tradition of Shillaber's Mrs. Partington. However, Whitcher did create a character who presaged Holley's feminist spokeswoman, a writer of woman's rights essays named Samantha Hocum. This character, although still a satirical figure in Whitcher's scheme, may have been the inspiration for Holley's eloquent feminist Samantha Smith Allen. Whitcher's work, which first appeared anonymously in *Neal's Saturday Gazette* in 1846, emerged just on the surge of demand for dialect humor, a wave of popularity on which Holley was carried for more than thirty years.

Two other women writers of the "feminine fifties" also lived and wrote upstate: Emily Chubbock Judson of Eaton, who used the pseudonym Fanny Forester, published *Alderbrook* in 1847; Sarah J. Clarke, born in Pompey and known to her readers as Grace Greenwood, had produced *Greenwood Leaves* in 1850. Both short fiction writers, they produced collections that were best-sellers.

Holley's vernacular humor connected the tradition of the women's sentimental novels and stories, which these women practiced within, with the later "B'gosh school" of fiction that Irving Bacheller, another North Country writer, explored and expanded. In his novels Bacheller drew as heavily as Holley on the dialect, manners, and values of the region, although he tended toward a more realistic mode of narrative than she did. At the other extreme are the stories of Philander Deming, Holley's contemporary. Born and reared in Schoharie County outside the southern boundary of the North Country, Deming drew heavily for his narratives on the habits and ethics of the people he knew from the summers he spent running a sawmill in the Adirondacks. As much in touch with the realities of upstate survival as Holley, he chose to etch in chiseled prose the harsh life of the upcountry. It was a fictional chronicle that Walter Edmonds in the 1930s continued in his upstate novels, blending the realism of Deming with his own strong narrative gifts.

Like all the North Country writers of the nineteenth century, Holley shared the sense that politicians were just neighbors and politics an activity as much connected with all their lives as farm chores and church meetings. Segregated from the rest of the nation by terrain as well as by choice, North Country people maintained a strong moral solicitude for the country as a whole and a willingness to pronounce opinion on political matters. The region had been a "germinating ground for politicians" from Cleveland to Roosevelt.[2] The presence of real political figures and the assumption that they would listen to the thoughtful women and men of the country informed much of the thinking and writing that came out of the upstate region.

In any encounter with a politician, Samantha takes it upon herself to admonish, congratulate, or advise him regarding his stand on the issues most important to her. When she goes into New York City in the first novel, it is especially to see Horace Greeley, who was to run for president. Although she admires him, she disagrees with him on "biled vittles, Wimmen's Rights, and cream biscuits," and she is determined to set him straight on the central matter at least. In the same way, she accosts President Grant at the centennial. He had earned Samantha's wrath by pressing the prosecution of Susan B. Anthony after she and sixteen other women had voted in the 1872 presidential election in Rochester, New York. She preaches to him for several pages before she concludes:

> And then I advised the Nation (through Ulysses) what to do in the great cause of Wimmen's Rights. I talked eloquent on that subject, and in closin' I drawed his mind back a few years to the time when a great war was goin' on between justice and injustice, and how God wrought out of it the freedom of a race, before He gave the victory. I reminded him that another great battle was goin' on between temperance and intemperance, and how, in that warfare, I believed God was helpin another race of human female beins to liberty; by showin' to man how He enabled *them* to win greater victories than had ever crowned *man's* efforts, and provin' what *they* would do for God and humanity if the power was given them.[3]

In this same manner, Samantha talks with many of the movers and shakers of the 1870s, trying to persuade them through her sturdy common sense to adopt her views on woman's rights and temperance much as her campaigning sisters actually buttonholed politicians during the century of petitioning for the vote.

The primary concern for Holley was to gain the ballot for women. Holley, like Philander Deming, had witnessed the toll on women of the desolate, painful, and fearful life in the rural districts of New York State. This made both writers sensitive to the plight of women, who held no political power. Irving Bacheller would likewise recognize the drudgery and hardship of farm and woodland life for women, but with his bent for nostalgia and pastoral idyll, he more often masked the reality with an aura of rustic sainthood, portraying the women as angelic, patient, virtuous mother-women. Elevated to such a pedestal, women were as powerless as ever to gain their fair measure of dignity and independence. Sainthood was not what Samantha or Holley sought. Against Josiah's argument that a woman's place is on a pedestal—to keep her from the polls—Samantha argues:

> I just as lives be on a pedestal as not, I'd kinder love to if I could set, I always did enjoy bein' riz up, if I had nothin' to do only to stay up there sometime, but wimmin have to git round so much it wouldn't work. . . . But that hain't the main reason I'm agin it, it is too tuckerin' a job for wimmin.
>
> Tuckerin' to be enthroned on a pedestal with the male sect lookin' up to you and worshippin' you. . . . How under the sun can I or any other woman be up on a pedestal and do our own housework, cookin', washin' dishes, sweepin', moppin', cleanin' lamps, blackin' stoves, washin', ironin', makin' beds, quiltin' bed quilts, gittin' three meals a day, biled dinners and bag puddin's and mince pies and things, to say nothin' of custard and pumpkin pies that will slop over on the level, do the best one can! How could you keep 'em inside the crust histin's yourself up and down?

To all of this Josiah angrily answers, "They could manage it if their minds wuz strong enough."[4] It is against that sort of logic and literalness that Samantha struggles in both the private and public domain. Samantha frequently insisted:

> I never contended that wimmen was perfect, far from it. You have heerd me say in the past, that I thought wimmen was meaner than pusly about some things. I say so still. My mind haint changed about wimmen, nor about pusly. But justice is what I have been a contendin' for; justice, and equal rights, and a fair dividin' of the burdens of life is my theme.[5]

Central New York State women already had developed a tradition of political activism and feminist unrest. Elizabeth Cady Stanton and Susan B. Anthony took up the cause of woman's rights, especially the right to the ballot, in Geneva in 1848. Frances Willard, head and heart of the Women's Christian Temperance Union, was born in Churchville, New York; Dr. Mary Walker, advocate of women's rights and a surgeon in the Civil War, was born in Oswego, New York. While these women carried on the work of campaigning for the vote by lecturing, petitioning, and convening, Holley used Samantha's voice to reach other audiences with the truth about the injustices and indignities of a woman's place in society. At the same time, Samantha chronicled the homely events and hard work that set the rhythm of life for country women: the domestic trials of planting and harvesting, cooking and canning, washing and sewing, often for a large household of children and hired hands. From her stories we know the ceaseless toil of farm life as well as the spirit and turmoil of life in a small New York State town not quite of the New England character but very like it. Holley's works clearly depict the realities and rigors of such a life and thereby give us a glimpse of a time and place that otherwise went largely unrecorded. Such attention to domestic detail recounted with both humor and irritation made her works enormously popular with women readers.

Although her humor appealed most obviously to the masses of women who supported popular fiction, it also reached the reformers who were struggling with their own advocacy of woman's rights and temperance, and stage adaptations brought the arguments of Betsey, Josiah, and Samantha to audiences in colleges, churches, rural districts, and the theaters of Boston and New York City. Holley's impact across the nation is difficult to assess because we have no methods, few reliable criteria, and no way of judging influence from popularity. Obviously one publisher thought that it was worth it when he advanced her $14,000 for her world's fair book in 1893. All the early works were quickly successful; their first printings soon sold out and several were translated into French. In 1887 her *Samantha at Saratoga* was the year's best-seller.

Soon Holley was sought out by leading feminists and temperance leaders, including Anthony and Willard. The woman suffrage movement, having been diverted by the Civil War and then divided by factionalism, sought her support. The temperance movement, having begun in the 1840s as a response to the position of women at the mercy of drinking men, informally merged with the woman suffrage movement under Willard's direction when she saw the vote as both a means and an end. Under the evangelical banner of Home Protection, women petitioned for local option. Suddenly more women were conscious of their political strength, and soon the Women's Christian Temperance Union represented more than two hundred thousand women in every state in the Union.[6] Holley was enjoined to appear with them, write for them, and finally even to tailor the Samantha novels to suit their goals by killing off Josiah. Clearly they believed in the breadth of Samantha's influence, as did clergy who petitioned Holley to write novels concerning their own reform strategies, most notably for the consequences of manumission in the South and the position of women in the Protestant church. So powerful was her influence felt to be that she was invited to address the United States Congress on woman's rights. Men who would not listen to a feminist speaker's arguments would read Holley's books with delight, accepting through her humor the subversive notions of suffragist thought.

The popular literature of the period from the 1820s to the 1870s was predominantly that of women writing for women, a body of fiction through which "American women became authors and readers." This popular domestic fiction was written by the likes of E.D.E.N. Southworth, Caroline Lee Hentz, Susan Warner, and Marion Harland as well as a horde of lesser-known writers, producing the works that outsold the literary output of Hawthorne, Melville, Thoreau, and Whitman.

Novel and short story alike relied on an overplot that affirmed for women a life-script they could pray and hope for, one in which a girl, beset by adversities, becomes a strong, happy woman. Typically, a young girl, abandoned or left without a guardian in the world, confronts that world, marshals all her talents and determination, and carves out a life for herself by asserting her right to make her own way, although most often the fiction ends in an appropriate marriage for her. The message seemed to be that through independence and self-reliance a woman could find ample use for her wits and her gifts, struggling to achieve a sense of selfhood along the way and participating in a new feminine heroism. With that attained, there was no reason to marry, although, in fact, marriage to a man who appreciated her strength of character was a kind of reward for her virtue.[7] Holley adapted the conventional narrative line and the didactic intention of these earlier writers to her own feminist and prohibitionist motives. In Holley's novels we see the young woman after the wedding, fourteen years after, when other tests of her character, stamina, and adaptability arise. To get the message of her more pragmatic feminism to as many women and men as possible, she wrapped it in the vernacular humor that the public had come to appreciate from Jack Downing and Frances Whitcher. Taking the notion of home-centeredness that the sentimental or domestic novelist had used, Holley turned it to her own purposes by taking up the life of one of these heroines after the marriage vows are said. Holley's Samantha books pick up the narrative well after the honeymoon, when cast-iron affection rather than passion has taken hold.

Taking the pragmatic, moderate feminism of the writers of

women's novels, Holley sketched the overplot, particularly in the characters of Tirzah Ann and Betsey Bobbett, showing the failure of the pink-and-white tyranny. After the Civil War, the "matrilineal piety"[8] of Catharine Beecher, Harriet Beecher Stowe, Sarah Orne Jewett, and Charlotte Perkins Gilman was an attempt to provide new heroines, role models for the late nineteenth-century readers. Holley sent forward the bustling, substantial, thoroughly indomitable farm wife, Samantha Allen. At the center of the stories Samantha presides, the antithesis of the genteel maiden, the maiden-turned-matron.

So Holley's Samantha stories draw on three literary traditions—the rustic humorists and literary comedians, the domestic fiction of the feminine fifties, and the emerging local-color movement—melding them in a unique way that no writer has since done. Like the vernacular humorists, Holley fixed her works in the voices of dialect speakers. But like the other North Country writers, Holley's work is also rooted in a sense of place. There is always an awareness of seasons and landscape even when Samantha is traveling through new territory. Holley is, in this way, a regionalist interested in portraying Americans who differ slightly in detail from other Americans rather than what is unique and picturesque. Hers is a democratic and panoramic vision of the nation, yet her work anticipates the women local colorists like Harriet Beecher Stowe, Sarah Orne Jewett, and Mary Wilkins Freeman in her depiction of the details of life in a circumscribed area, a single district of New York.

The manners and customs as well as the quirky speech of the New Englanders who settled the North Country are plainly recorded in the novels. The cycle of socials and church services that sustained the upcountry folk, the domestic scenes, the rustic voices all record a life in the near-wilderness of the upper regions of New York. Deming was sketching the harsh, cramped life of the North Country in stories less like Holley's than Jewett's and Freeman's—taut, lapidary prose pieces with little of the dialect and none of the humor of Holley's work. It was not until Irving Bacheller recreated the Yankee settlers and their habits of speech and being that the Yorker dialect humor was again heard in fiction. By the time Irving Bacheller's *Eben Holden* was published in 1900, Holley was nearly worn out with the crusading spirit that had fortified Samantha. Bacheller, espousing lesser reforms, picked up the thread of vernacular humor and local color that Holley had spun.

Like most of the women local colorists, Holley treated both the grim difficulty of country life and the hardship of domestic care, but hers was a vision tempered with laughter. Like the others, she also created a fictional community of characters: Jewett sketched Deephaven, Rose Terry Cooke depicted Bassett, and Holley described Jonesville.

Like them she also worked best in the short forms. Her novels are typically sketches hung together on a thin narrative strand that often keep the same characters. Unlike the sentimental writers who viewed hearth and home as an attitude as much as a place, the local colorists and Holley have in mind a very fixed place and a sense of rootedness. Holley's works remain centered at the Allen hearth even when, in the later works, Samantha is launched on her travels and everything is compared to home but suffers in the comparison. Holley and these writers take the sentimental heroine forward, retaining her sense of independence and self-reliance, often to eccentricity, but showing her alone and childless, often telling her story herself.

Holley begins to seem like this heroine come to life. As others have noted, there appears to be a pattern in the lives of popular women writers of the nineteenth century. Many were widows with children or single women with families to support. Disclaiming any literary aspirations, these women had the better excuse for their literary ambitions—writing out of economic necessity. Holley's situation is consistent with the pattern. She came from a modest background and never truly wanted a public life. Her father had belonged to the farming class that was rapidly losing status. Her life was one of retreat as she remained single and celibate, choosing to live in rural New York State most of the time, using her childhood home as a base. She was perhaps uncommonly devoted to her mother. As with many of the other local colorists, she did her best work early in her career and outlived her reputation.[9] Like Whitcher, Holley was a retiring sort whose avoidance of public life incurred the charge of haughtiness. Like Jewett, Holley was accused of being critical of the culture that had nurtured her, a charge that was a misunderstanding of her sympathy as well as her devotion to accuracy of detail. Holley's was a life of ambivalence and conflicting images: public acclaim and private loneliness, urban gentility and upstate rusticity, maidenhood and marriage, poetry and prose, art and life, snow and roses. Her creative reconciliation of these disparities makes hers a life worth scrutiny.

With the surge of feminist energy in academia, Holley's works are being republished and read. A one-woman show of Samantha's best "episodin' and allegorin'" by Jane Curry, titled *Samantha Rastles the Woman Question*, brings the humor and the character to a new generation of audiences much as Hal Holbrook does Twain's. This biography is a part of the new enthusiasm for Holley's work and complements the studies that are being made of her writing and the work of other nineteenth-century women writers.

However, my search for her life was both professional and personal. As I was growing up near her home in northern New York State, Marietta Holley was just a quaint and ancient-sounding name on a marker in the churchyard. People in those parts sometimes gave directions by telling how far a spot was from "the Holley place." Nevertheless, Holley was remembered as a local character rather than as a writer. We never read her fiction in our schoolbooks. Her novels were not to be found in the village library. The stories that remained were anecdotes about goings on at "Holley's Folly" as the house was called. The blue-and-orange New York State historical marker that stands along the roadside in front of her house was merely a curiosity. I grew up hearing the fictions surrounding her life; I aim now to set forth the facts of her living.

I

WOODLAND AND FARM

Admit the fact, own up that the little soul hain't a part of your own life, but has a separate life of its own, with its own duties, pleasures, cares and rights. It has a right to its own little thoughts and ways, its own little likes and dislikes, and the best we can do is to teach it to stand alone and stand straight. . . . A tough lesson for mothers to learn, one of the toughest and hardest, but it is right.

—Marietta Holley, *Samantha Vs. Josiah*

IT'S ONLY A GIRL. . . ." Thus were the births of female children recorded in the local newspaper during Marietta Holley's childhood in northern New York State. Her own birth in the summer of 1836 at the family cottage in southern Jefferson County went unreported for lack of a newspaper at all. The seventh and last child in her family, Marietta was born into a life of labor on the farm that her grandfather and father had hewn out of the New York State wilderness with their own axes. The strip of land that lies between Lake Ontario on the west and the Adirondack ridges on the east was a low, nearly level plain coursed by clean, spring-fed creeks. Rich with cedar forests, pinewoods, and wildlife, the land tempted settlers like David Holley, Marietta's grandfather, to hack through the timber to secure a place after the turmoil of the Revolution. David left Connecticut with the promise of government bounty land for his service in the American army.[1] On the trek up the Mohawk River valley, through Oneida County and finally, in 1807, into the region of Bear Creek, he brought with him his sightless mother, wife Sarah, three sons, and two daughters.[2]

What the Holleys found when they arrived were blind paths through the woodland and small patches of cleared land where other New England families were setting down roots for the next generations, building rude huts, and bearing their children. All the land was suitable for grazing if not for planting. The fertile soil was underlaid by a limestone layer that formed humpbacked outcroppings on the higher ground. The going rate for land was three dollars an acre, with the obligation to clear two acres and build a dwelling within a certain period of time.[3] David's sons—John Milton, David, Jr., and Cornelius—were young and vigorous. With their brawn and the women's fortitude, the family soon had opened a building lot on a natural terrace east of the path that led north from the Bear Creek settlement. When the land was cleared, it offered a dry, protected base for their log home with a view in the distance of the grey waters of Lake Ontario eight miles away.

The countryside surrounding their farm was marked by the remnants of long-gone Indian encampments. As other settlers cleared and dug, they discovered the mounds, trenches, enclosures and artifacts that mutely told them of the struggle for survival in the North Country. A few rods below the spot where the first house was built lay a cedar swamp haunted by wolves, as was much of the region then. By 1815, the bounty on wolves had gone up to fifteen dollars.[4] Wolves as well as panthers were ominous presences in the lives of the women, which were a contrast to the comfort and security that they had left behind in Connecticut. The daughter Sylphina, "young, and pretty, and missing the society she had left," was probably not consoled by her father's insistence that she "cheer up . . . you may live to see a road cut through the woods here."[5]

In fact, she did. The path widened and deepened into a roadway until by 1814, partly to assist the war effort, the plank road north from Salina (now Syracuse) to Adams village was opened and christened Salt Point Road.[6] By that time Lemuel and Sarah Taber had arrived in Bear Creek from Rhode island with their young family, which included their daughter Mary.[7] "Squire" Taber was justice of the peace for Bear Creek. An educated man, he taught classes in higher mathematics, surveying, and astronomy.[8] Like David Holley, Lemuel Taber had served in the Continental army and had been caught up afterward in the migration of other Yankee settlers toward the freedom and opportunity of the Oneida region. He moved on, stopping when he met the Vermonters who had come across the northern route, down the Black River valley into south Jefferson County.[9]

The Tabers' girl Mary seems to have adjusted more easily than

Sylphina Holley to the rigors of living in the Ontario district. Mary eventually passed on to her own children the pride of survival and a spirit of perseverance, binding even the youngest of her children in a powerful tradition of Yankee fortitude. Many years later her daughter, Marietta Holley, would recount with awe the story her mother told her about riding to Henderson Harbor, thirteen miles away, for supplies. She had been caught in one of the fierce thunderstorms that crash in off the lake, but she made her way home with her baby tied in her arms and the goods slung over the horse in a knapsack. Marietta relished her image of "the dark forest, the young wife trying to find her way in the dark lit by lightning flashes, and vocal with cries of wild animals."[10]

Such stories of heroism were the stuff of the children's lives. The times were dangerous. It was a frightening, painful life with the specter of early death for the women of Mary's generation. They endured the loneliness and physical hardships as well as the certainty that not all their children would survive. Compounding those ever-present threats, the War of 1812 burst upon the countryside. Mary Taber's activities during the war years are undiscoverable, eclipsed by the part the young John Milton Holley and his comrades would play. John enlisted[11] and served the cause by volunteering for "the carrying of the cable," a display of heroics that still survives in the stories that grandparents tell their children in Jefferson County.

In May 1814, a load of arms and riggings needed to ready three warships that were being built at Sackets Harbor was ambushed en route from Oswego. The waterways had to be abandoned; the mud-filled roads were nearly impassable. The militia decided to attempt the overland route through the forests, so the cannons and lighter riggings were unloaded from the boats and reloaded hastily onto small wagons and horses. The last item in the inventory was a 9,600-pound cable that was at least 750 feet long. No wagon was large enough or strong enough to transport it. With the danger of another British attack increasing, volunteers stepped forward to shoulder the cable. Soldiers and citizens, 250 of them separated only by the distance of a man's stride, bore it the twenty miles to the outskirts of Sackets Village where the navy met them, relieved them, and carried the rigging triumphantly into town.[12]

It was just one more incident in the heroic lives of the Yankee pioneers, one typical tale of bravery, self-sacrifice, and patriotism which the Holley children were reared on. A simple creed was a constant for their generation. It was expected that one's life would be hard, a long series of difficulties that only ingenuity and perseverance in the faith—whether in one's country, one's sect, or one's self—could overcome. The lessons were stern, but the children learned them early and well.

When John Milton returned to the homestead from the war, there was need of another house on the Holley land. John, then thirty-three, was to wed Mary Taber from Bear Creek. The bridegroom's father, to keep the family together, divided the land among his sons, giving David and John each a parcel and helping them build their own homes. John and his father erected a small frame cottage at the foot of the terrace and opened a section of land for a large garden. On 8 May 1817 John Milton Holley brought home his twenty-one-year-old bride Mary to begin their forty-six years together. It was a lean, cramped, sometimes hungry existence. The families grew together, forming their own small settlement of kin related by birth and marriage. That first year was marred by the death of John and Mary's infant son Jerome Bonaparte, but there quickly followed other children: Jerome Brightman (1819), Dewitt Monroe (1821), Sarah Angeline (1823), Adelia Sylphina (1825), and John Milton, Jr. (1828). The farm was growing as John inched out more and more land, claiming it for tillage. Besides supporting his own brood, it provided him the means to acquire a little more property. In 1835 he had two other small farms, which he let on shares. By the close of that year John had "fifteen acres of improved land, two neat cattle, two horses, eleven sheep, seven hogs, and sixteen yards of fulled cloth woven during the year past and eleven yards of woolen not fulled."[13]

Then Mary was pregnant again. Her health had been very poor, but the local doctor insisted that having another baby would improve it. From her eldest daughter Angeline's account, it seems that Mary truly loved babies, and—because it was easier to become pregnant than not—she was expecting a child in the summer of 1836. She was forty years old.

On 16 July the last Holley was born. As the mother lay near death, expecting it, she named the girl Marietta. Perhaps she had used up all the family names with the boys and Sarah and Sylphina. Perhaps in giving the girl the diminutive of her own name and no middle name at all she hoped desperately to keep alive her matrilineage. She called Angeline, who was then fourteen, to her bedside and gave her this charge: "I have named your little baby sister Marietta, and I give her to you and want you to promise you will love and care for her as if she were your own."[14] Somehow, probably through her own will rather than any medical skill, Mary's health began to improve. The relationship between the mother and the tiny daughter was forged into a bond that was stronger even than that with the rest of the family. Mary and Marietta grew together and lived together all Mary's life, with Marietta acting out a devotion and affection that was at once dutiful and yet freely given. Mary in her turn protected her youngest as best she could. The child was small and a girl, handicapped by her health, her sex, and later a speech impediment. To Mary, her last child was never "only a girl." She was her mother's pride. Although often Mary did not understand precisely the talents Marietta had, she always defended her right to exercise them. At the same time, the mother struggled to fit this new child into the farm family.

The Holleys were clearly a hard-working unit. As was usual in the rural districts, the boys attended school sporadically when they could be spared from seasonal imperatives like planting and harvesting. They were a boisterous group, the house always bustling with nieces and nephews from next door and frequent visits from Uncle Dave. He was a charming raconteur with a flair for a turn of phrase, apt metaphor, and quick pun.

All the Holleys enjoyed discussing politics and religion. They delighted in a good argument at the supper table after a day's work on the land. The local paper published in Adams, only three miles away, began appearing in 1844.[15] In addition to the neighborhood and county items, obituaries, and birth notices, the paper brought news of national and international excitement and issues.

The Holleys had no pretensions to being anything other than simply hard-working, honest Christians, but their enthusiasm for language, politics and a good story kept them in touch with the world beyond their own precincts. They had invested in the country as equal shareholders. Their naive belief in a classless society was beginning to give way by 1850 to an awareness that a self-styled elite was growing up in the village of Adams. Gradually the ideal society of the postrevolutionary period was becoming "increasingly stratified and self-conscious."[16] The elder Holleys seemed untroubled by the emergence of those genteel folk from the rural background. They could even laugh at some of their pretensions. Uncle David said "he always put on his 'Loathing suit'" when he went to Adams to visit his sister Chlorinda and her husband Whitcomb the jeweler because "they were too high hat for him." He had a clear sense of himself as a rustic clown. His stories, filled with homely incidents and images, must have infected the child Marietta. He punctuated his conversation with homestead humor, such as protesting that he would have to leave for home precisely at nine o'clock so that he could turn the hired girl over because she began to snore at nine. The little girl's leisure hours were filled by his stories as well as pioneer tales, village gossip, and political debates that constituted the family's entertainment during the evenings and long winters.[17]

Marietta's place in the family gatherings was a difficult one. Being the youngest by eight years, she was truly the baby. Besides, she was a frail child. She did not walk until sometime after her second birthday and then only by hanging onto her mother's skirts. She was prone to fainting spells, even as a toddler. When she began to talk, her speech was impaired by a lisp. She was innately a timid character who was happiest at a slight distance from everyone but her mother. She needed to establish a place of her own in the confines of the farm cottage. At night she even drew away from her parents in the crowded bed they shared, pulling herself up to the headboard away from them as far as possible before she could fall asleep. As she grew older, she was content to withdraw into herself, away from the activity of the household to occupy herself with her drawing and scribbling. As she remembered her childhood, "Though money was always scarce and we lived in the simplest way, we were never in want for the necessities of life, and I had abundant time and leisure for reading, scribbling and drawing pictures, which was my great recreation at that time, for I meant to be a great artist."[18]

Of course, there could not have been unlimited leisure because Marietta attended the district school about a mile and a half away, at least until the fourth grade.[19] Furthermore, the females in the household were busy with the routine work of keeping the men, the sons, and the hired hands fed and clothed. Mary and her daughters also tended the large garden; preserved what foods they were able to; and finished all the spinning, weaving, knitting, quilting, and sewing they could. Textile manufacture was crucial to the economy of the farm. The girls materially contributed to the family by earning a bit of money or increasing their bartering credit at the local stores. Marietta knit mittens that she carried down to the store in Bear Creek to trade for commodities that the farm could not supply, just as her mother and sisters traded eggs, butter, apples, and woolen socks.[20] That kind of domestic industry was valued by the family as much as the men's labor. When Uncle David could no longer ride horseback or do the heavy farm work, he learned to knit socks because "no self-respecting man . . . would sit with folded hands."[21] So the rhythm of their days was regulated by mealtimes, seasonal chores, and housework. They snatched whatever private time they could. Marietta spent hers writing as soon as she learned how. The knot of women seems to have encouraged her in this, helping her keep secret her scribbles. The boys, as much older as they were, were alien to her. She insisted that they loved her, that they would "cheerfully have risked their own life [*sic*] if I had been in any bodily danger,"[22] but they loved also to plague her. She made an easy target because she was by nature and by habit a shy creature who blushed easily. Her lisp was a source of great pain to her when they mocked her speech. Perhaps because Marietta went to school more than they did, the boys would bait her by asking her to recite or spell a word and then laugh even when she did so correctly, turning the supper table into a public horror for the girl. Long after she would remember, "At the table my brothers had only to point a finger at me, or say meaningly to one another, 'Look at her,' when the slow painful blush would arise."[23] It must have been to some degree a relief to her when she was virtually alone with her mother and sisters after the boys left home about 1850.

Moved by the same pioneering spirit that brought their grandparents to Jefferson County, the brothers headed west. Jerome Brightman, whom the family called Bright, left for Montana while the other boys, Dewitt and young John, started for the goldfields.[24] They no doubt realized that the farm could not support all of them. The whole region had changed from a wilderness to a stable farming district: the patriots and pioneers had truly settled. Their children had moved forward into the century with a naive optimism. The landscape was rapidly changing. By midcentury there was a telegraph line through Adams. A railroad line was completed from Rome to the settlement that had been Bear Creek. When William C. Pierrepont moved there and built his rather grand house, the name was changed to Pierrepont Manor.[25] The hamlet was growing rapidly into a village at the intersection of two railroads. Eventually it had several stores, an inn, a post office, and forty or fifty dwellings.[26] Three miles in the other direction, the village of Adams was similarly burgeoning into a town. Gen. S. D. Hungerford, soon to become an important character in Marietta Holley's life, had opened his bank in the village. A female seminary had been started with Miss Willard (who was probably either the daughter-in-law or a niece of the famous educator and woman's rights advocate, Emma Willard) brought from Troy to take charge of it. The main street had an opera house, called Saunder's Hall, which could seat one hundred people.[27] The leading lyceum speakers of the day were booked to speak to crowds that included the business people of Adams as well as the farmers of the surrounding area. Without the price of admission, Marietta often missed the likes of Henry Ward Beecher, Schuyler Colfax, and assorted temperance advocates, although she read accounts of their lectures. As years passed, when she could afford to go or was invited as an honored guest, the lectures at Saunder's Hall introduced her to the notables of the abolition and suffrage movements, as well as to lecturers on some merely quaint and exotic features of midcentury Americana such as phrenology, galvanism, mesmerism, astrology, spiritualism, and so forth.

Meanwhile Marietta continued going to the district school. In very bad weather she boarded with an uncle who lived close by. It was at this school that she met a woman who profoundly shifted the direction of her life by being a model of the independent, assertive woman she wished to be. There was a young schoolteacher boarding around the district, a woman with a "slight, erect figure and plain, determined face" and a name long since lost. Wherever she went to board, she carried with her a package of bran, which was a most unusual habit but one that Marietta emulated as she grew older. This schoolmarm quit teaching to become a book agent, a vocation that required her to go door-to-door in the backcountry selling books by subscription. For a woman it was difficult and unseemly work. It was hardly more respectable that she wrote a book about her experiences on the road and went back out to sell that book. In addition to all that, she was an avowed spiritualist.[28]

Spiritualism was an ardently debated issue in that part of the country. The rural folk took their religion very seriously. Eventually that region would be part of the "burned-over district," which was so called because of the frequency and intensity of revivals during the first half of the nineteenth century.[29] At one time the district had more spiritualists than any other region in the United States, while New York State as a whole had twice as many adherents as any other state.[30] It was a popular movement, especially suited to the rural rather than urban areas. In southern Jefferson County it excited debates that usually ended in the resolution that something genuine was going on, but its source was unknown. Marietta was a sensitive, impressionable young woman when the schoolteacher suggested the possibilities of spiritualistic communication to her. The idea fascinated her, developing into a conviction that she never totally abandoned.[31]

The schoolmistress' concern with diet and health similarly impressed the girl. Marietta knew early that she was somewhat frail, and she was often stricken with upper respiratory ailments. Like all the other Holleys, she was slight of build and very agile, "able to vault fences and climb trees like a squirrel."[32] Still, she recognized the precariousness of her health and began a lifelong regimen to protect herself by eating, dressing, and exercising conscientiously, even fastidiously. It was an age of enthusiasms, whether for following the dietary rules of Sylvester Graham or for table rapping that followed the public displays of the Fox sisters in western New York State.[33] With her inclination to be different and emulate the teacher, Marietta was quickly caught up in the new ideas.

The nameless schoolmistress' most important gift to Marietta and American literature was the realization that a woman from her own sphere could write a book. The girl had been sketching since she could hold a pencil. She later wrote "little stories, poems, descriptions of people, scenery, places"[34] for her teacher, but she kept her writing hidden from others except her mother. She was, by her own admission, an indifferent student.

> I had a passion for learning everything, but not through hard work and steady application. I did not like that, but gleaning every bit of knowledge that I could that came easily. Astronomy, botany, French, drawing—all had their turn, passionately followed for a time, and filling my waking moments. . . . I was wont to scribble verses when I should have been trying to master the multiplication table (an instrument of vague torture to my mind) and fill any blank pages with faces more or less resembling the human countenance. As my dresses grew longer so did my scribblings increase.[35]

Paper was at a premium, so she kept and used every scrap that she could find and her mother could salvage.[36] She used her father's discarded account books to write her verses in. Someone who saw the old books reported that "the journals of 1808 to 1836 are hardly legible now [1936], for every square inch of space was written on and even the records were written over." When nothing else was at hand, she wrote on the back of leftover wallpaper.[37] Her parsimony continued long after there was need for it. About 1880 she was using an old copy of the *Patent Office Report (Agricultural)* for 1852–53 for a scrapbook. Over its pages she pasted newspaper clippings about her and her work, snatches of fiction, bits of humor, and poetry by Lowell and Milton with marginal comments. In the front is a pencil drawing of two stern profiles that look remarkably like a young Josiah and Samantha, the "pardner" and his writer-wife who form the focal point of the Jonesville circle in the Samantha stories.[38] Even when she no longer needed to write to support the family, when *Samantha at Saratoga* was selling hundreds of thousands of copies, she hoarded paper, making good use of every bit. An old proof copy of *My Opinions and Betsey Bobbet's* served as a journal where she jotted down curious names for characters ("Berthena, Calferna, Dalfina, Latiza, Albina") and anecdotes for use in other stories.[39] In the early years she saved paper by writing in a hand so tiny that it could hardly be read, squeezing about twenty words to a line and putting two lines of manuscript between ruled lines.[40]

Paper was not the only thing the family lacked. When Marietta was fourteen, there was no more money for her schooling. With the boys gone west to make their fortunes, the girl was needed to work on the farm. She kept up her share and even helped to absorb Angeline's after she married D. Page and moved to her own farm a little way off. A near neighbor who had a daughter about Marietta's age recognized the girl's abilities and sparkle and continued Marietta's education informally by giving her private lessons in botany and various other disciplines. The woman and the two girls stole time to wander through the meadows and woodlands, mixing lessons with long walks. These times stood out in bright relief against the grinding work of the farm. Another nearby family had what seemed like a large library, although it was actually only a set of bookshelves hung on a wall. They gave Marietta and her sister Sylphina free use of it to satisfy their need for information and hunger for words.[41]

The reading matter in the Holleys' own home was meager. Their father had become a Universalist when the revival that swept over the district in 1821 had won many converts and culminated in the organization of the Universalist Church in Ellisburgh close by.[42] In those spare years there were few books or periodicals in the house other than the Bible, the *Universalist Magazine*, and the *Gospel Advocate*.[43] While the Tabers and the rest of the Holleys stayed in the Episcopal Church, John Milton Holley went his own way. In spite of their differences in religious practices, the whole family agreed about the various reform movements, especially temperance and abolition. As a Universalist, John had that "tender conscience, the intense concern for the community, and the preoccupation with a perfected society" that characterized that sect.[44] Around the supper table the family argued the merits of various reform strategies with John very likely taking the temperate course that would lead to practical improvements. Such moderation was instilled early in Marietta. Her fictional characters are often ridiculous in proportion to how far they deviate from this "megumness" (mediumness or pragmatic moderation). That was the creation of a mature woman, however; in the mid-1850s Marietta was still a young woman with emerging sensibilities and passions. On the brink of her womanhood, she was confronted with the limitations her station put on her aspirations. Facing a life of marriage, children, and responsibility for her aging parents, she was looking at a life script that threatened her with early death, a violation of her very private self, and the end of her dream of writing.

In this period of transition with all its tensions, she was drawn to the Baptist revival meetings. They had begun with Elder Jacob Knapp's evangelism in the 1830s.[45] The unstudied eloquence of an evangelist's extemporaneous preaching excited the country folk. North Country farmers distrusted high-flown rhetoric whether in politics or religion.[46] The fire of feeling that swept across tent meetings may have caught the imagination of the girl who was used to her Uncle David's cool Episcopalian worship and her father's calculated Universalist belief. Very likely the girl saw in the strong female societies within the Baptist organization a place where she could fit. Women had full liberty to participate in all the Baptist meetings except for formal Sunday services.[47] The evangelical religion "nourished the formation of a female community," one that was "both a resource and a resort."[48] In it women could find an identity as spiritual equals and a purpose that transcended the routine necessities of making a living. By 1853 there were twenty-six Baptist churches in Jefferson County.[49] One of them took Marietta Holley into its congregation.

Her conversion took place at Giddings Schoolhouse scarcely two miles from her father's farm. The revival meetings had begun in autumn when the harvest was over. They had been going on for several days, lasting late into the night with no results that could be counted. Finally, sixteen-year-old Marietta quietly rose and simply asked for everyone's prayers. The "slender girl with a pale, serious face" was the first converted that year in a revival that lasted throughout the winter.[50] It took an enormous effort—or an intense spiritual power—for Marietta to speak out in that public way. Years later when writing about her natural timidity, she commented that it was reticence which made it

> so hard for [me] to talk about intimate things. . . . When I united with the church, and Heavens knows I was in earnest, it was almost a physical impossibility for me to rise and tell about the struggles and victories of my inner life. So hard was it indeed that when I tried to do what others did and rise up, it would seem as if the seat would come up with me. It seemed too sacred and too much of a secret between my soul and the All Highest to talk about to brother and sister mortals.[51]

Like most of the deeply personal events of her life, her conversion is partly concealed from us by her intense need for privacy. Much is hidden, alluded to, but never spoken of directly. There are many absences and silences in her biography, particularly concerning her family. Her father is strangely missing from the pictures of the Holley hearthside. Stories of Uncle David, the brothers, her mother, even the hired boys run through her autobiography and her novels, but beyond the fact of his religion, we know little else about him. He liked to play checkers in the evening, maybe while his brother David was telling his stories.[52] He kept a blue cup of muscovado sugar at his place at the table, giving a child an occasional taste.[53] As quietly as he had lived, he died without notice at his farm in 1861. His passing did not even merit an obituary in the Adams paper.

The years following the death were especially difficult for the women as they tried to keep up the farm with little help from the uncles and in-laws who could hardly spare anything themselves. The Civil War stripped the countryside of the able-bodied men, so the Holleys could manage to keep only a boy around to help with the chores. Marietta's hopes must have been nearly extinguished by the care of those hungry years, but the love of beauty was a light that her mother tended as best she could. The girl loved music, but there was no money for lessons or a piano, until one of her uncles overhead her singing one day. He commented to Mary that "her voice [was] as sweet as a lute, and she ought to learn music." He gave Mary the money required for one term of lessons. To practice, Marietta had to walk to the house of the teacher until her mother rented "a jingling old piano" from a relative who was moving away. The girl was diligent in her study, improving rapidly until she graduated from the country music teacher to a more sophisticated one in Adams and finally to a "professor" in that town. Soon she was giving lessons herself in her mother's house.[54] The best way for a young woman of little means to earn money in private teaching was to offer "accomplishments" to girls who aspired to gentility.[55] By 1870 Miss Holley was giving private lessons to young ladies at a rate of eight dollars for a course of twenty-four lessons, at one time having as many as eight pupils.[56] A traveling salesman offered to sell her a parlor organ or melodeon in a rosewood case. At that time a cheap piano would have cost about three hundred dollars and a melodeon about a third of that.[57] Going against the dark forecasts of the neighbors who said she'd never pay for it, Marietta had the melodeon placed in the front room. Soon not only had she paid it off with her earnings from teaching, but she had struck a deal with the piano agent to receive "a generous commission" on every instrument that her students bought.[58] It was only the first business deal that Marietta contracted. She clearly had a shrewd sense of her own abilities by then, and thirty years later when she was making substantial deals for the sale of her manuscripts, she eschewed having an agent make her arrangements, preferring to negotiate and handle the bids herself. Although her naïveté sometimes led her into contracts that neither bound nor protected her, most often she got precisely what she wanted, as she did with the melodeon.

The money she made from giving music lessons eased the family finances a little, but the struggle to meet expenses went on. There is little evidence that the brothers contributed very much during the period after the father's death. Only one letter survives, from Bright in Virginia City, Montana, dated 18 August 1864. Addressed to his dear little sister Ette, it recounts his adventures in the goldfields. He speaks of earning four thousand dollars a day. Laborers were paying eighty-four dollars in gold for a bushel of potatoes. One passage describes in detail a hanging he had witnessed, which was one more example of the extravagance and lawlessness of the Western wilderness. He continues, "When I think it is safe I will send more money," then confides his plan to return to the farm the next fall. It appears that he did not return but made his way through Montana into Arizona where he took up law.[59]

Bright was probably Marietta's favorite brother: he is the only one to whom she wrote a poem that was published. In October 1863, before Bright's letter, the verse "To My Brother J.B.H." by "Ette" appeared on the front page of the *Jefferson County Journal*. The poem is conventional in its imagery, but there is genuine pathos in her picture of the sister and brother sitting together at evening singing. That vision is contrasted to the girl's days now, which were full of domestic care. The poem concludes with the mother calling to her to stop writing and go to bed, but before she breaks off, the poet plaintively asks when the brother will come home. The poem is one of the few pieces of Holley's published works that has clear autobiographical content. Because of that, it is a curiosity from a woman who was normally so private about her life.

Without much assistance, Marietta held what was left of the family together. The teaching she did was acceptable to them as a genteel and respectable occupation. She needed their approval as well as the money that teaching brought in, so she continued with it even as writing became more and more important to her. Through the 1850s and 1860s she wrote mostly poetry. The few prose pieces of that period are only sketches and anecdotes, some in Yankee dialect. Most of her writing time was snatched away from her other responsibilities, usually in the evening. She spent those hours in a room behind the best room in the farmhouse, struggling with her muse. After years of success, she remembered:

> How far off those days seem, when alone, but not lonely, I sat in the small cottage room and wrote and wrote and rewrote! And looked through the lilacs and roses that grew about the low window, and saw beyond the long green fields the sunset behind the drooping elm, and saw what Youth sees, what Hope sees, . . . the blue mountains of my desire.[60]

As her confidence in that desire grew, she was determined to send off a poem to the Adams newspaper. Each week a poem by a well-known poet such as Lydia Hunt Sigourney or Henry Wadsworth Longfellow appeared on the front page. In great secrecy, not even confiding in her mother, she sent off two poems signed Jemyma. She did not dare to tell anyone for fear that she "could never, never endure the ridicule if . . . rejected."[61] To her amazement, the editor accepted both poems to appear in the 23 July 1857 issue of the *Jefferson County Journal.* When the newspaper arrived at the Holley house, an uncle with a literary bent lauded the poem "Welcome to Summer," which appeared on the front page.

Welcome to Summer

Welcome sweet summer, welcome back to us,
Is thy fair smiling face with roses crowned;
And emerald robe loose floating in the air,
And waving curls with loveliest jewels bound.
Yes loveliest jewels, sweet forget me nots,
And star-like anemones and violets blue
And pale, pure water lillies, in whose radiant cup,
Like radiant diamonds drop his pearly dew.

Welcome glad summer long has been the day,
Since we a farewell sighed to thy departing step;
Yet dear and sacred in our inmost hearts,
A memory of thy beauty we have kept.
When autumn winds were wailing through the grave,
And dreary winter's storms burst on the air
Thy graceful form would gently 'fore us rise
And from the contrast seem doubly fair.

Welcome gay summer, yet amid thy smiles,
Some tearful memory's will sadly rise,

Of hopes and joys once ours in summer days,
As calm and peaceful as the cloudless skies,
They rise before us in our reveries
With their old blessed hallowed gleam;
And we forget what mournful memory tells us,
How their light faded in a broken dream.

Welcome bright summer, so sweet voices greet thee
In every hall and cottage, hut and bower;
I'll not forget that step the first to greet thee,
The voices that gushed forth in a music shower.
She met thee like the birds with songs of gladness,
She parted from thee with tearful eyes,
She'll meet thee not again, for sighing,
We'll point the drooping willow 'neath which she lies.
She'll meet thee not again in this dark changing clime;
But where thy splendor, fadeless and eternal,
Lives on, unbroken by the flight of time.
Where endless summer shines upon the wreath
That angels are twining around her brow,
Its leaves will fall not in the dreary autumn,
Beneath no blighting tempest bow.

Welcome sweet summer with thy joyous train,
Of dancing sunbeams and zephyrs gay,
And dreamy twilights and dewey flowers,
And all things beautiful THAT CANNOT STAY.
Yes, that's the shadow darkening all it's glory
And ringing in our hearts a solemn bell,
That soon to all its lights and beauty,
Our lips must murmur farewell, farewell.

Only after Marietta was confident of the sincerity of the family's praise did she reveal herself to them as the Jemyma who had produced not only that lyric but the light verse on an inside page of the same issue.

Phair and Phalse
affectionately dedicated to all unfortunate lovers

She was phair as rosy shadows,
on a bank of virgin snow.
She was phair as Yankee sausages,
or sunset's dying glow.

She was phair as a pure and snowy cloud,
on the brow of evening seen.

She was phair as the heart of a wild rose bud,
or a dish of pork and beans.

She was phalse as whispered vows that on
the breath of even dies,
She was phalse as hollow onions,
and "emptins" that won't rise.

But though phair and phalse, sweet creature,
Your image will ever be,
Shrined in this faithful heart of mine
to all Eter-ni-tee.

So at twenty-one, the same age her mother was when she married, Marietta saw her first work in print. It was a tentative beginning. Some of the neighbors were critical of her initial venture, finding it difficult to believe that the girl they saw "feeding hens, gathering apples, and even climbing trees, could possibly write anything worth while."[62] She was, after all, only a girl, and a local one at that. Thus began the estrangement between Marietta and her rural neighbors. It was a separation that she tried to heal as she grew older and more famous, but one that was never really reconciled. Her mother always took Marietta's part in the conflict. There was one particular woman who prided herself on having her domestic tasks finished before anyone else. Toward that end, she kept a watch on the chimneys of her neighbors' houses to see when they were up and about. Once she appeared at the door with the observation that they had arisen rather late that morning, and she wondered if anyone was sick. Mary replied that Marietta had been up late the previous night finishing a story, and because she had to walk the mile and a half into Pierrepont Manor to mail it later in the morning, Mary had kept the household quiet to let her sleep. At that the neighbor launched into a scornful lecture on Marietta's duty to support the fatherless family. She insisted that the young writer would never make enough to pay for postage and paper. She added that she knew of a widower who wanted a hired girl to help him with his two children and fifteen milk cows. Marietta could earn three dollars a week and "if she suited him he might marry her. A poor girl don't get a chance like that every day." With the patience of a woman who knows she's right, Mary countered, "God has given her a talent as you will see some day and I could not live without her."[63] Unable to speak out in her own defense, Marietta depended upon her mother's support, encouragement, and protection.

2

HEARTH AND GARDEN

You see I have come out in my right name. . . . When a person gets famous, there ain't no use in concealin' their name any longer; it looks affected.

—Marietta Holley, "Borrowing the Magazine"

IN THE VERY NEXT ISSUE of the *Jefferson County Journal*, Holley's first piece of prose appeared. Titled "Piety," it was a trifling little story about a Mrs. Howard whose concern over the religious observances of her neighbors is juxtaposed to her own fussing about whether her new silk dress with its fashionable furbelows will out do the gown Mrs. L. had worn to Sunday service the previous week. The story is essentially a monologue directed at her maid Minna while the girl helps Mrs. Howard dress. In it the woman takes pious swipes at Elder Honeytongue as well as at a neighbor whose faith is suspect because he actually digs potatoes on the Sabbath.[1] In a single piece, Holley addressed many of the subjects she would continue to wrestle with for the next sixty years: the vanity of fashion, work over worship, the value of class status, the absurdity of the "cult of true womanhood,"[2] the evils of drink, and the importance of staying close to the land. At the same time she had found her most effective mode: a single strong female voice speaks against one or two other—usually contrary—voices in a rather static situation. There is a good deal of talking and philosophizing going on, but little movement. In this regard, Holley's speakers were much like the popular Yankee monologists who used simple irony and understatement to elicit a chuckle from their audiences.[3] Like most of the early stories that followed it, "Piety" is merely a sketch rather than a fully developed short story. What Marietta really wanted to work at was her poetry, always feeling that "though expressing myself in prose for awhile, still poetry was more worthwhile."[4] Her prose was the re-creation of the common voices she heard around her; poetry was the expression of her own singing voice. One was work, the other art.

Over the next two years Marietta was a regular contributor to the poetry column on the front page of the Adams newspaper, but the writer's identity was hidden under the name Jemyma. Why she chose that nom de plume she seemed not to know exactly, though in part it was an act of rebellion: "Heaven knows why I took that plebian name, unless it was as a revolt at the fancy names, the Jenny Junes, the Minnie Myrtles, and Fanny Ferns."[5] The fancy, alliterative names were not only too whimsical for the sensible Marietta, but too flimsy: "I recognize how inappropriate such youthful names become as writers grow old. With this in mind I first wrote under the name of 'Jemyma,' which I felt was plain enough and strong enough to sail on triumphant to ninety, if need be."[6]

What she does not acknowledge in that prophetic comment is her concern for maintaining her privacy and keeping her writing a secret from the community. The name Jemyma had no apparent connection with the Holleys or Tabers, so it provided a shield for Marietta's identity. Like other Yankee writers, Holley often favored biblical names for their ironic or tragic significance as well as their comic overtones.[7] The allusion to Jemyma, one of the three daughters of Job, may have been a reference to Marietta's being the third daughter of a hard-working Christian.

Most of the neighbors knew nothing of the young woman's writing career. Judged from outward appearances, life continued routinely at the Holley place. It seemed Marietta's time was spent giving piano lessons and helping to manage the farm labor. Her writing time was restricted to the quiet spaces in the farm business when her mother could intercede to make time for Marietta to attend to her newly important work. Although she received no pay from the *Journal* for her poems and bits of prose, she continued to work at refining her skills as though anticipating a day when her writing would provide her economic support. That the writing had to be fitted in around the duties of the farm and music room is clear from the pattern of publication over the period from 1857 to 1873. Few pieces appeared during the summer and early autumn months—the busiest seasons on the farm. Most of the publications cluster in the midwinter months and cease to appear in mid-May. The habit of writing intensively during the long winters was one she soon established. Winter in the North Country came early and lasted late. First snow often appeared in mid-October, and the brutal temperatures and storms continued until the countryside was so thoroughly covered that the last trace lingered until May. In deepest winter snow drifts twice a man's height blocked the roads; trains were stopped and passengers stranded for a week at a time; no mail could get through. Farm families might be isolated for days until a neighbor could plow through with a team or someone could get out on snowshoes to pick up supplies, mail, and news. Being snowbound was a very real and hardly a romantic hardship for the Holley women.

Forced to rely entirely on themselves and (after John's death) whatever boys they could keep around the place, they struggled against the season and wove a comfortable solitude about themselves. Mary was in her sixties, reasonably healthy, and still capable of her fair share of the homestead labor. Sylphina was a ghost in the house; no one other than her mother and sister saw her. Marietta rarely mentioned her sister Finy. For those outside the family, it was as though she did not exist. Neighbors told of seeing her for a moment at a window, with the curtain drawn back a bit, but the lace would fall like a veil as soon as the figure peering out saw that she had been noticed. Unexpected visitors to the farmhouse would hear a bustle and know that Sylphina, caught unawares and unable to escape upstairs, was hiding behind a drape in the sitting room. Although the sister Angeline and her husband would often invite Marietta's household over for "an extra good chicken dinner at noon," Sylphina would never go along. It seems she never left the house; no one saw her in the garden, yard, or pasture. Some still say that the reason for her oddness was a tragic loss, that the man she loved had been killed in the Civil War, and she had never recovered from the shock of his death. The story, charming, romantic, and true enough for too many women in the country, was concocted in spite of the facts about Sylphina. When the war began she was nearly forty years old and, like her namesake aunt, already a spinster. The family's explanation of her aberration was that she was simply "peculiar from birth" and that "she could not help her peculiarities." Her only relationships were with her mother and Marietta. Slim and good looking, she favored the Holleys in her features, and like all the rest of them, she relished a good argument about politics when she and Marietta disagreed on the issues—and they often did. Despite their differences, the two sisters shared a love of history and the "good literature" of the day: Dickens, Thackeray, Eliot, Hugo, Hawthorne, and, of course, Shakespeare.[8]

This odd little household continued moving with the rhythm of the work to be done. Sylphina and her mother kept the house in order and domestic industries going while Marietta maintained an income from the properties and her teaching. The youngest woman struggled with the cares she complained to Bright about, the dulling necessities of working at hearth and henhouse.

A little poem, published in June 1862, titled "Duty and Beauty," describes the tension between wanting to pursue the arts and needing to make a living. Two sisters, Mary and Arminta, are sketched as respectively representing homely duty and aesthetic pursuits. The poem concludes that the poet must give in—but not give up—and live in this world as well as the rarified atmosphere of poetry:

> But an eye for beauty should descend
> From clouds and tender gloom,
> Sometimes lie down the poet brush,
> To wield a mortal broom,
> Sweep down cares crumbling embers
> And sweep the parlor hearth,
> And make the dear home fireside
> The brightest spot on earth.[9]

For Marietta, home and her mother came first, always.

The two pieces of farmland let on shares by "time servers" did not produce much, "only weeds and troubles." Although it was no longer necessary to fight to keep the wolves from the front door, there was the strain of hiring and managing a succession of hired hands. Becuse they could not afford a man's wages, the Holleys picked up a boy however they could, sometimes giving a job to a troubled youth who needed shelter and the influence of a stern but warm Christian household. The adventures and trials that the women had with this assortment of boys prompted Marietta to comment that she could write a splendid book about them that might well be called *The Acts of the Boy*—"which are far different from the Acts of the Apostles." Their "bright, stupid and mischievous" faces and scamps' ways delighted the young woman, although she never did write the book. Stories of their malingering, reluctant churchgoing, messiness, tale-telling, and other harum-scarum ways punctuate the novels and stories she did write, while beneath them lies her appreciation for the fun, the sheer pleasure they took in being children.[10]

One particular boy named Lyman was the product of the hasty marriage of a local man to a woman of "shady reputation" in Chicago. The boy became a street urchin until his father finally returned to Jefferson County and offered the boy as a worker on the Holley farm. In spite of his shabby dress and too-wise looks, Marietta took him on. He had a slight peculiarity of speech and an amazingly wide but not "choice" vocabulary. Marietta admitted that it was "a temptation not always resisted to make him say long words (which was his delight) in his quaint way" and that she even eavesdropped on him as he said his "Our Father" at bedside in his room at the top of the kitchen stairs. As the object of torment herself because of her lisp, Marietta was sensitive to Lyman's handicaps. She encouraged him to learn his lessons, took him to Sunday school in a suit the women had made out of discarded adult clothes, and put up with his pranks. In spite of all she did, there was a sense that blood would tell, that—especially after his father returned to claim him—Lyman's chances for ever being more than a scalawag seemed slim.[11]

Still the urge to reform was strong in the Holleys. Soon after Lyman's departure, an older boy, Joe Fields, was brought to them by a lawyer friend who had defended him in a petty theft suit. While living with his aunt, Joe had allegedly stolen a breastpin from her, but the lawyer believed he had the potential for good if only he could be given "kind treatment and good advice." The women found him to be a hard worker who never stole a penny from them. When his father abruptly appeared after a few months to take him away, they felt it as a loss to both Joe and themselves. Within days a hardware store in nearby Pulaski was robbed. Joe's father was arrested; Joe got away. At nightfall he appeared at Marietta's door looking "more sinned against than sinning." Although she might have been suspicious of his connection with the robbery, she took him in.[12]

At three o'clock in the morning a commotion and loud knocking at the front door wakened the women. After considering whether they should even respond, Mary bravely called out to ask who was there. The rough voice on the other side of the door announced itself as "the law," but a more refined man's voice assured them that they need not be alarmed, because they were only after Joe Fields. When Marietta let them in, the constable hustled upstairs to seize Joe and the missing goods. Marietta pleaded with the young hardware merchant to let him off, but the constable insisted that it was a second offense, and the boy must be prosecuted.

Joe was sent off to a reform school for a year, but as soon as he was released he turned up at the Holley's again, the only place he had known kindness. This time Marietta recognized a change in him, a sinister look, the lineaments of a criminal. Though she pitied him, and it hurt her to do so, she closed the door on him, and he vanished.[13]

The young hardware merchant was not so quickly disposed of as the boy, however. Within a few days of the arrest, he went back to the Holleys—in daylight—to apologize again for having frightened the women so. Before he left that day, he asked if he might call again. For several weeks the man's overcoat lay on the hall chair during his frequent visits while Marietta and its owner chatted in the parlor. Ella, Marietta's young niece from next door, played about the house poking into things, including the coat pockets. There she discovered a purple velvet box containing a dainty gold watch and chain that was probably intended as a gift to Marietta. She showed the treasure to her grandmother. There was a desperate discussion in the parlor, and after that the young man from Pulaski did not come to call again.[14]

Other suitors followed, but Marietta was vague or secretive about who they were and when they courted her. She was a good-looking young woman, slight, with chestnut hair that naturally waved about her face. Her features were not quite plain, the nose a little more Roman than she would have liked, but her eyes made up for any deficiencies in any other part of her appearance. They were deep brown in color, but that was incidental to their appeal. People who met her could not tell you what color her eyes were, only that they held you with a look, invited you to tell her everything you thought or felt, mesmerized you with their fire and excitement, made you laugh with the glint of merriment there. Without speaking more than your name, she could draw you into conversation and reflection with those eyes. It may have been those qualities in her look that attracted the man from Pulaski. Fame added to her charms as the years passed, and other men offered her marriage, but her commitment was to her duties as she saw them: her mother and sister first, then her writing. At the close of the 1850s she was struggling to write and publish much more. At twenty-three, she began to sign her work Miss M. H. rather than Jemyma. It might have been a weak signal to the limited world she knew that she was finally ready to declare herself as an artist. For that her initials would have sufficed. Using Miss before them seemed to announce her confirmed status as maiden lady or spinster. As she felt more confidence in her poems, she ceased hiding behind her initials; by the end of 1859 she was published as Miss Marietta Hawley, using the English spelling of her father's name and retaining the Miss.

The commitment to her craft was a conscious denial of other commitments. As she saw it, she could not marry and still do all she aspired to. In the latter part of her life, she reflected the ambivalent feelings that

> Heaven only knows why I never married. I only know that when the situation became imminent, and got to the stage of "take me or leave me," it was always esier for me to take the latter course. But my heart was touched sometimes and my feelings lacerated, but yet more than once with the tears in my eyes I was able to turn my back on care and matrimony. . . . The wave of attraction . . . turned the other way and washed me high and dry on the shore of Celibacy.

> There are many reasons that conspire to clip the wings of Cupid, a perhaps overstrained sense of duty to those dependent in a way for support and companionship and the inborn love of freedom that rebels at being bound by even Love's golden chains are some. . . . And Art is a jealous mistress and one who follows her would do well to weigh the question well before setting up another rival.[15]

With such considerations, Marietta suggested there might be fewer "unhappy literary marriages"—or simply fewer marriages. In a light verse, "Lament: On the death of fifteen infant Geese, the author's only earthly possessions," written in 1861, the artist mocks love letters and lovers' vows, drawing a contrast between "matrimony's cruel sea" and "single life's fair shore."[16] For a personality as timid and private as hers, the intimacy of marriage must have seemed indeed threatening.

During this early period her circle of friends widened as the village of Adams became the locus of her professional and religious life. The editor of the Adams newspaper, W. J. Allen, was her supportive friend and publisher. In 1858 she had joined the Adams Baptist Church, where she sang in the choir.[17] As her little renown began to increase so that readers recognized her as the poet Marietta Hawley, she attracted the attention of Gen. Solon D. Hungerford, one of Adams' leading citizens. He swept her into his melange of businessmen, clergy, literati and local squirearchy. Twenty-eight years older than Marietta and married, he was handsome and dynamic, a gentleman. His appeal to Marietta included his ardent patriotism made manifest in his own service to the country throughout the Civil War. As she did, he had faith in the future of the Republic so long as its citizens adhered to solid, simple values. Furthermore, they shared their farming roots. Having been born on a farm in northern Jefferson County, Hungerford had never lost his love of the land and farm creatures, even though that love had taken on a very modern attitude in his concern for breeding procedures, the newest and best methods of doing anything, and agricultural progress generally. His Valley Park Farm with its racetrack for thoroughbred horses and pastures for his prize Ayrshire cattle was a grand complex of farms and gardens.[18]

Hungerford's bank was doing well, as were his interests in the railroad, so he could turn his astonishing energies to improvements for the village and to a genteel social life. As a local dignitary he with his wife Ann entertained the lyceum speakers, giving teas and receptions for guests such as pulpit orator Henry Ward Beecher, Vice-President Schuyler Colfax, and General Sherman. It was at these gatherings that Marietta met those and other notables. Beecher and Hungerford had become acquainted in August of 1859 when Beecher spoke in Adams. While in town, he visited Hungerford's farm and purchased for his own herd two heifers and a bull.[19] When Beecher returned the next June to deliver his lecture "Politics and Religion," Hungerford used his influence as a director of the railroad to get a special car to transport to the lecture a party of his friends, in which Marietta was included.[20] Beecher, brother to educator Catharine Beecher and writer Harriet Beecher Stowe, was "an object of reverence and almost worship" to her then. Nineteen years later, when Theodore Tilton lectured at Adams, the allegiance to Beecher was still so firm that Marietta scorned Tilton socially, although she attended his speech. Tilton had instigated the scandalous lawsuit on the charge of adultery against Beecher in 1874 and so had tarnished his reputation. Ignoring the evidence that Beecher was guilty, Holley chose to see Tilton as the villain. She refused to be introduced to him or to acknowledge him at the afternoon reception that they both attended.[21]

Other gatherings and teas provided the setting for Holley's meetings with important feminists and suffragists. Although Marietta was only twelve years old when Elizabeth Cady Stanton and the others gathered at Seneca Falls in 1848 to declare their grievances at the Woman's Rights Convention, she certainly knew about the fever in the wind, the emerging feminist consciousness. Living as she did amidst a tangle of women, dealing with the world as the head of the household, holding the abolitionist sentiments that were linked so closely with the feminist movement, she was inevitably taken up with the ideas of the women's movement once exposed to them. In September 1859 Susan B. Anthony and the Reverend Antionette Brown arrived in Adams on their way to begin meetings for Jefferson County on civil and political rights.[22] Anthony was increasingly well known throughout the state as the organizing force within the women's movement and the complement to Stanton's philosophical bent and eloquence. Because she was unmarried, she was free to travel about firing up feminist sentiment into active support. Brown, the first woman to be ordained a minister, was accompanying her at this particular stop. Generally woman suffrage was an unpopular issue in the township. The first editorial on woman's rights in the *Jefferson County Journal* did not appear until 1871.[23] "The Woman Question" was belittled in jests and advertising as well as in the way local women continued to be identified in the columns of the local newspaper. Birth announcements still often read "It's only a girl at the ——— house." The birth of a son was heralded by an announcement that the man was the proud father, but there was usually no mention of a mother or of a woman's being involved in the birth at all. Married women were listed in social and legal notices by the professional or occupational titles of their husbands: Mrs. Dr. Minar or Mrs. Rev. Saxe might have presided at a Presbyterian tea; Mrs. Editor Johnson was visiting out of town. One running advertisement capitalized on the prevailing bad feeling about the suffrage movement, mocking its significance and sincerity: "The Woman Question—how shall I trim my new hat? Answer—call on Mrs. L. J. Bullock."[24] The reform impulses that galvanized the county for abolition, that made it unnecessary to draft soldiers from the local townships because enough men enlisted, faded before the issue of woman's rights.

For Holley, the outbreak of the Civil War was the public calamity of 1861. Her father's death was a private one. Having buried him from the farmhouse, she set about organizing her life to accommodate her new responsibilities. She had no near relatives in the fighting, so her concerns about the rebellion were only empathetic, although no less genuine. The war hardly appears in her work. She presented to the Pierrepont Manor Debating Society an eloquent essay on abolition and manumission during the winter of 1862, but other than that and three poems that appeared in the *Journal* during that year, she seemed to feel the war as a distant conflict. One of the poems, "WAR," recounts the death of a noble soldier but returns repeatedly to the image of his daughter waiting on a hillside in Maine for him to come home. It was a man's war but a woman's suffering that Holley rendered. Although she recognized the magnitude of the war as a threat to the Republic, woman's rights occupied her imagination more often.

The following May 1863, a sketch titled "Gipsy and I" appeared in the *Journal*. The central speaker, Miss Jessie, was invited to a neighbor's for tea to share a new book. Leaving the pet lapdog Gipsy behind, the maiden lady went across the lot where the women settled in for a little reading and a good deal of talking about their real concerns: cooking, rearing children, religion, and slavery. Jessie is the forerunner of Samantha Allen; she is eloquent, thoughtful, patient, and shrewd. Unlike Samantha, she speaks in what Holley liked to call "good English" rather than the rural New York State dialect. There is even in this story a wrongheaded husband who intrudes on the women's sensible discussion of the slavery issue. The spouses' disagreements over every aspect of every question force Miss Jessie to retire to the quiet of her own window seat and patient pet. The literary and satiric possibilities of matrimonial discord had become clear to Holley. The way was ready for the emergence of Samantha and Josiah Allen, but the first of the Samantha novels was yet ten years in the future. Marietta considered herself a poet rather than a fiction writer, so she directed her energies into her verse.

With growing confidence she began to seek from acknowledged poets assurance that her work was good poetry. Like Emily Dickinson's urgent questions to Thomas Wentworth Higginson asking if her verse was "alive," if it "breathed," Marietta's letter to Henry Wadsworth Longfellow begs attention as well as appraisal. Along with this letter, she sent the sentimental lyric "Isabelle and I."[25]

> I hardly know how to apologize for writing you. If I should say that I loved your poems *so well*, that by right of that I could address you without fear—how many could plead the same excuse for if every one whose heart has been touched tenderly by your writings should write you—you would be inundated by leaves of notepaper. I will not try to justify myself, but trust to your kindness to pardon the liberty I am taking in writing at all and the favor I write to ask, I will try and have the merit of being brief.
>
> I live in the very depth and solitude of the country and nearly all the people around me though very kind and sensible—still poetry is to them, what Paul's preaching was to the Greeks, "foolishness," and so it happens that I have hardly one to whom I can talk about that which interests me most, and so I want to ask you—is there any *poetry* in the verses I enclose? I know the lines are of about equal length, and rhyme—but I mean is there any *real poetry* in them. You will know at the first glance, and if you will take the trouble to read them—and write me just a few lines giving me your opinion I will be more obliged to you than I can ever tell you. I have enough poetry or verses to make quite a large book. They are most of them quite long pieces, and they are better I think than the shorter ones—but they are too long to trouble you with—and after all, the pieces I enclose are quite fair specimens of what I am able to do in authorship. I know you are wearied with letters asking your criticism, but I will try and not tire you with the length of mine.

If Longfellow ever replied to this plaintive request, his answer was lost because Marietta never recorded it in her autobiography or kept a copy in her papers. Still needing responses to her work from those she admired, she sent other poems to Lydia Hunt Sigourney and Oliver Wendell Holmes. Marietta thought Sigourney "stood at the head of American letters" because her work appeared so frequently in the press and was included in a little book of poetry that Sylphina had acquired.

Many of Marietta's published poems up to 1864 were maudlin death poems in the style of Sigourney, often about the demise of a "Little May," occasionally concerning the early death of a local child. Very likely Marietta sent two of these to the aged poet. Sigourney was nearing the end of her life, writing her autobiography, when she replied to the twenty-eight-year-old Holley's letter and verses with faint praise and the injunction to do good with her talents.

> I am happy to say to you what I am not always able to say to those who solicit literary criticisms—that you undoubtedly have the gift of poetical powers and that your cultivation of them reveals prosperous attainment in the somewhat difficult structure of English verse. I, therefore, in conformity with your request, offer you encouragement in that intellectual department, and wishing you success and that you may ever keep in mind the good that it may be in your power to do by the impressment of right principles and feelings, I remain, . . .[26]

This stilted scrap of encouragement kept the younger woman writing, although there was a shift away from the mourning poems after this time. In part that might have been because of advice received from her cousin Henry W. Holley, who himself had a taste for good writing. Much later Henry would make a name for himself as an editor, publisher, and politician in the Midwest. His sound literary judgment was obvious even as early as this period when he urged Marietta to write stories rather than verses and essays.[27] At about the same time she received a similarly pragmatic letter of advice from Holmes, to whom she had sent two poems. He responded that they showed "a practical talent . . . which may by cultivation produce good fruit." He advised her, as he did other young writers, to "adopt a characteristic signature and publish a few [poems] now and then in the best paper or magazine" that would accept them—if she felt she must publish at all. After telling her not to be discouraged, he concluded:

> Cultivate all your gifts, the practical one with all the rest, read the best English models, and the few American ones that may be found. So perhaps our "Marietta" will by and bye crown in among the shining ones, and have the magazines asking for her instead of knocking at their door for entrance.
>
> But do not let the time given to practical composition interfere with any duty, or encroach upon the time which is best devoted to that study which forms the basis of all true excellence.[28]

Feeling charged by these reactions, she summoned the courage to begin sending her work to magazines. In the spring of 1867 *Peterson's* magazine accepted her poem "The Haunted Castle" to appear in the April issue.[29] Her patience and persistence were finally beginning to bring her some compensation. Soon she had sent *Peterson's* two sketches that she had developed into short stories. "Fourth of July in Jonesville" appeared in the July 1869 issue and bore Marietta's new pseudonym, Josiah Allen's Wife. Like many of the vernacular humorists before her, she opened her narrative with a letter to the audience, Peterson himself. The epistolary mode had proven successful for Artemus Ward and Josh Billings, so Marietta chose it as a genre suited to her purpose—to demonstrate the fun and fervor of a patriotic celebration in the rural districts of upstate New York. True to her perception of herself as a writer, however, she mixed in two poems with the delightfully accurate prose sketches of local charcter types and manners. Thus was born Samantha Allen, née Smith, Josiah Allen's Wife.[30]

Holley might have chosen a male pseudonym as some of the English women writers had, but the women's voice was too strong and her message too feminist for such a masquerade. Holley was coy about why she chose that name, sometimes saying she did not know or that "it was an original name that no one else would be likely to want."[31] The fact is that the Allen name belonged to one of the first families to settle Bear Creek, the Joseph Allens, as well as to her friend, W. J. Allen, the editor of the Adams newspaper. Locals felt she had compromised them in some way by choosing names associated so clearly with the locale. Nevertheless she continued to do so in her Samantha stories and the novels often using the names of neighboring families, their abrupt syllables jostling each other in a way that echoed the Yankee lingo: Adsit, Spicer, Tuttle, Widrig, and Wart.

When she considered more carefully the question of a pen name, she admitted that "probably I thought it would soften somewhat the edge of unwelcome argument to have the writer meekly claim to be the wife of Josiah Allen and so stand in the shadow of a man's personality."[32] It was a prudent literary choice. The themes she was working over were temperance and suffrage, unpopular issues that could lead a zealous reformer into preachments and sermonizing. By disguising the noble idealist and radical thinker as merely a man's wife, she was luring the unwary reader into expecting a treatise by one of the Antis, or "Auntys," as Samantha called them, not some uppity woman like Margaret Fuller or a reformer like Harriet B. Stowe or even a scribbling hothouse Fanny Fern. At the same time the pseudonym protected Holley's privacy, thus allowing her to live quietly in her neighborhood without having to continually argue her message or live out Samantha's fictive life for others.

The first venture with *Peterson's* brought in thirty dollars, which she deposited at Hungerford's bank in Adams. Never having been in a bank before, she was full of awe as though "at the center of great financial affairs." When the cashier noted the publisher's name on the check, he asked if she had been "getting up a club for the magazine." With her usual reticence, she answered merely no, leaving it to him to ponder how the young woman came to have dealings with a publishing firm. Keeping this little secret from him—and her neighbors—delighted her. She continued to send out her stories and sketches, but with them went her poems. In 1870, remembering her meeting with Beecher, she sent "God's Summer" to the *Christian Union* where he was editor. He accepted the poem for publication, sending a modest sum with a note praising her "sweet little poem." So intense was her admiration for Beecher that she valued the compliment more than the cash.[33] The family had been used to bartering for whatever it did not produce, so an increase in the use of cash in the farm affairs was new to Holley. She cautiously deposited the monies she received from writing stories for the magazines while her poetry was put aside. During 1869 no poetry was published at all in the *Journal*. The paper had a new editor, S. R. Pratt, who had a wife who wrote poetry amid the jumble of a young family. Her works began to appear in the spot where Holley's had previously been seen until the winter of 1870 when her two daughters died of scarlet fever. She and her husband moved away to Carthage where she became coeditor with him of the Carthage newspaper in 1873. With that literary rival gone, the way was cleared for Holley to continue publishing locally, but after her success with *Peterson's* and the *Christian Union*, she could no longer afford to publish for nothing what she could sell.

She saved carefully until she had enough to purchase a coal stove to replace the inefficient wood-burning one in the sitting room.

Her mother's bedroom opened off this room, and it pleased Marietta to overhear her mother telling her neighbor how the new stove heated her room so thoroughly that she needed to keep her arms out from under the covers at night. The money from writing bought more "comforts and conveniences" for her mother. With the pleasure of a child, she delighted in knowing that in "those days of small things . . . I spent my money first in making my mother comfortable instead of buying the fine clothes and adornments for which my soul longed."[34]

Her brief encounters with the social whirl of Adams whetted her appetite for elegant and fine accoutrements, but she always returned to the plain farm cottage taking comfort in country pleasures like the rose-laden lattice at the cottage door.

However fierce the winters in the North Country, the summers were a delight to be savored. The weather was unpredictable, to be sure, with the mercury rising as much as forty degrees over a single day and sudden thunderstorms rolling out of the west, but the women could visit friends, neighbors, and relatives at a distance. Those ventures and the pleasures of garden and hayfield brought with them a summer sense of freedom and expansion. Even though the farm was busier in summer, Marietta could sometimes use the lengthening daylight to polish her prose and practice her poetry and still get the garden terrace cultivated and the hens fed.

Her neighbor's bitter prediction that Marietta would never make enough to pay for postage and paper had been proven false enough, but she still had to walk or beg a ride to Pierrepont Manor to post her manuscripts. In 1871 she had saved enough to buy a sorrel pony and a small open buggy. An investment of ninety-five dollars bought her the whole outfit—whip, harness, lap robe, and all. With the new mobility came a new satisfaction, not being dependent on others to take her butter, eggs, and apples to market or herself to the post office.[35] Furthermore, she was free to take her mother out for drives on a whim, wherever she wanted. Terrified of horses, Marietta nevertheless learned to manage the pony, although it was the only rig she ever drove.

Feeling bolder and more self-confident, she ventured further into the publishing world. She put together a packet of manuscripts to send off to Elisha Bliss of the American Publishing Company. Bliss was already publishing Mark Twain, Bret Harte, and Josh Billings, and Marietta realized the reception a few pieces from an unknown author like herself might warrant. She expected rejection, but still she sent him a poem, a chapter of the expanded "Gypsy and I" written in her "good English" (with the spelling regularized), and a sketch in Yorker dialect by Josiah Allen's Wife. Feeling she was risking nothing, she boldly asked him if he wanted her to write a book for him.

His response was immediate: yes, and begin at once. He wanted more of the dialect of Samantha. Terribly disappointed, Marietta answered by return mail that she much preferred the style of the serial "Gypsy and I," that it had more literary merit and charm. To persuade him, she enclosed reviews clipped from the *New York Home Journal*, where the story had appeared. In spite of her entreaties, Bliss was firm. Even though his directors and even the author herself were uncertain of the work's value, he overrode all objections. When Holley's determination or inspiration failed, he urged her to continue, assuring her that the work would be a great favorite with everyone.[36] Bliss knew what he wanted.

His instinct for what would sell had proven to be profitable for the American Publishing Company. Before Bliss's tenure there, the company had published works with a "heavily evangelical cast," which did not do well in the marketplace. Bliss went about recruiting a different kind of writer, inviting Mark Twain in 1867 to write a book based on his European travel letters. When the company's directors balked at publishing the manuscript, primarily because they thought that its proposed title (*New Pilgrim's Progress*) was blasphemous, Bliss threatened to resign and publish the book himself.[37] The ploy worked, and a compromise with Twain allowed *Innocents Abroad* to be published as one of the two books the American Publishing Company brought out that year.

Such wholehearted support for his writers and their products made his company one of the most prosperous subscription book companies of the time.[38] After the Civil War there was a great boom in book sales by subscription as thousands of demobilized soldiers without stable employment were available as book agents. Door-to-door canvassing, getting the books directly from the publisher to the reader, was a sure method of increasing sales. The agents were persistent and persuasive; it was difficult to say no to a man who camped on the doorstep. By this method agents could sell thirty books for every thousand residents in a town, reaching folk who would never venture into a bookstore.[39] Bliss's success with Twain's book was enormous. Extravagantly illustrated with 234 woodcuts by True Williams, the book sold for $3.50, clothbound. When it was first issued, agents were selling nearly four thousand copies a month.[40]

The popularity of the wisely naive character that Twain created had been established in American literature since the christening of Brother Jonathan around 1800. In his incarnation as a Yankee type, the character appeared in plays all over the sprawling countryside from 1825 onward.[41] The characteristic shrewdness, the homely comparisons, the laconic responses to queries had appeared in the Maine letters of Jack Downing (Seba Smith) beginning in 1830 and the campaign doggerel of Hosea Biglow (James Russell Lowell) in 1846.[42] The rustic Yankee had appropriated to himself two literary modes that allowed him to pitch the drawling cadences of his speech to hold his audience until he was ready to deliver the punchline. The letter and the monologue—so seemingly simple, so artless, and so direct—were well suited to the Yankee's habit of giving his audience only as much as he was willing to let out, then abruptly shifting directions, juxtaposing images and sentiments for a wonderfully comic effect and always maintaining the appearance of not knowing how hilarious he had been. Holley adopted the style in her first book and successfully carried it through all the Samantha stories. In *My Opinion and Betsey Bobbet's*, Samantha Allen expounds on political self-reliance.

> I am not one to shet up my eyes and walk up blindly and hang on to anybody's apron strings, not even Horace Greeley's, as anybody can see in the matter of biled vittles, Wimmen's Rights, and cream biscuit. To think you have got to believe every thing your party does seems jest so unreasonable to me, as it would when you go out to pick greens, to pick skunk cabbage because cow cabbage is good and wholesome. Why skunk cabbage is pison, jest as pison as sikuta or ratsbane. Now the doctrine of free love as some folks preach it up, folks in both parties, why the smell of it is jest as obnoxious in my political and moral nostrals as the smell of sikuta is, and if anything smells worse than that, I don't want to go near it. Pick out the good and leave the bad is my theme in greens and politix.[43]

Like Holley's works, Jack Downing's letters from Maine, written in Down East dialect, continued for twenty years. Through irony and understatement he achieved his satiric effects. Downing disassociated himself from party politics, although he did act as confidant to President Andrew Jackson. That gave him free rein to poke fun at anyone whom he thought deserved it, regardless of party affiliation. In the West, Artemus Ward (Charles Farrar Browne) began his literary career with the publication of his 1857 letters that commented on current events and the sentimentality in the culture.[44] Petroleum V. Nasby (David Ross Locke) followed the style of Artemus Ward with his "decorative orthography,"[45] wrenched grammar, malapropisms, and anticlimax. Nasby's position as chaplain to the president and pastor of the "Church of the Noo Dispensashun" gave his character a twist of hypocrisy as well as a reason for the revivalistic cadences and mock oratory that he employed. Nasby's work was humor with a moral goal: wartime propaganda.[46] In this he and Josh Billings (Henry Wheeler Shaw) varied, though Billings mined the same vein as Ward and Nasby. His adaptation of the Yankee tradition was more aphoristic than those that had gone before, a style well suited to his *Allminax*.

In 1846, Frances Whitcher's Widow Bedott appeared, first in *Godey's Lady's Book*, the popular women's magazine, and then in her collected works, which appeared in 1856. Even though Ann Stephens was the first American woman to write vernacular humor, she had not used a female narrator.[47] Whitcher created America's first comic female figure of any import. Previously women had played no significant role in American humor.[48] Humorists had merely used conventional female comic types with "native idiom and idiosyncracy" added.[49] Benjamin P. Shillaber had limned a female speaker in the character of Mrs. Partington, but he had created a fool to be laughed at rather than a satiric figure to be taken seriously. Neither Bedott nor Partington was concerned with politics per se, although Whitcher used the widow to point up the absurdity of the culture's genteel ideal.[50] In the flourishing Down East humor of the period from the 1830s through the 1850s, Widow Bedott found her audience. Like Holley's Betsey Bobbet, the widow was desperate to marry, to work in "wimmen's spear," and to write dreadful sentimental verse. Her Yorker dialect, small-town background, concern with domestic detail, and sharp character delineation exemplified many of the down-home qualities that the male Yankee comics had, but to that list she added a portion of mother wit, a characteristic similar to the old New England "faculty." *The Widow Bedott Papers* were comfortably successful: the work went through twenty-three printings and sold 100,000 copies between 1855 and 1865.[51]

Close parallels between Whitcher's and Holley's work suggest that Holley was very familiar with her writing.[52] It is likely that Holley had read parts of *The Widow Bedott Papers* because it was customary in the North Country to share magazines such as *Godey's* and books such as Whitcher's when families could not afford to buy all the reading matter they wanted. It is equally as likely that Holley was familiar with the works of Artemus Ward, Josh Billings, and Petroleum V. Nasby because they were excerpted for publication in the local newspaper. These "literary comedians" continued the tradition of humorous expression by concentrating on verbal comedy and "acrobatics of language." From them Holley borrowed several tricks: misquoting Scripture and the classics; making incongruous catalogues; and using puns, mixed metaphors, anticlimax, and cacography.[53] Holley had been born at the time when "the American comic sense was coming to its first full expression."[54] She had grown up while the tradition flourished in literature and on the lecture circuits. At the same time she lived among local yarn spinners who imprinted on her young sensibility a regard for the peculiarities of the rustics' language and oral literture. It only remained for Holley to pull these strands together and create a female character who would not only make readers laugh but suggest workable, commonsense solutions to the problems that she satirized.

By the time Elisha Bliss read Holley's manuscripts, the rage for rustic comics was abating somewhat. Harriet Beecher Stowe and the women local colorists were beginning to look back with nostalgia. They wanted to recapture provincial characters that were rapidly vanishing rather than celebrate Yankee types.[55] At the same time, they felt the impulse to break away from the sentimental celebrations of the domestic novelists.[56] Thus the height of Yankee dialect humor was past, but the publisher saw in Holley's work an opportunity to continue reaching the readers in the rural districts who still enjoyed Yankee comic writing.

With a commission to write a book, Holley began to spend her days writing, sometimes working late to meet her deadlines. She often slept poorly and stayed abed as late as duty (or a neighbor) would allow. When her determination or inspiration failed her, Bliss would urge her to continue. She wrestled with her "reluctant muse," believing that the sensible, quirky prose of Samantha was unworthy and would never bring her the acclaim that her "fine writing" and poetry would.[57] Bliss made several trips to the farm to confer with her; he maintained a steady flow of encouragement through his letters. Finally the manuscript was finished. Characteristically, "with a little of Samantha's common sense and foresight,"[58] she had kept the fact that she was writing a book a secret from everyone other than her mother and sister, even from the relatives who lived just across the way. Bliss appeared in Pierrepont Manor to settle the last details of the book's publication, hoping to have it out in time for the holiday buying season of 1872. When everything seemed secure, the question of the title arose. The author had intended for the work to be called *A Beacon Light*; the publisher thought *My Opinions and Betsey Babbet's* was a better title. A compromise was finally reached so the book could appear: *My Opinions and Betsey Bobbet's: Designed As A Beacon Light, to Guide Women to Life, Liberty and the Pursuit of Happiness, but Which May Be Read By Members of the Sterner Sect, Without Injury To Themselves Or The Book.* A printer's error had changed "Babbet" to "Bobbet," and so it remained.

Marietta was on her way to the Sandy Creek Fair on the August day when the check from the American Publishing Company arrived. She and her niece Ella stopped off in Pierrepont Manor to pick up the mail, found the check in it, and hurried back in triumph to show it to the family. Here was proof that cousin Henry's advice had been sound. The first six hundred dollars from *My Opinions and Betsey Bobbet's* added to the little pleasures and comforts for Marietta's mother—an extra bit of lace trim for her caps and a new morning gown perhaps. Holley made a trip to Adams to buy presents and survey the goods of the local jewelers. Remembering one of her mother's favorite maxims, "Win gold and wear it," Marietta returned to the farm cottage having bought for herself a gift: a fine gold watch and chain.[59]

3

HER PLACE IN TIME

But in the words of the sammist (slightly changed), there is a time for visitin' and a time for stayin' to home. A time to neighbor, and a time to refrain from neighborin', a time to talk, and a time to write sermons, wash dishes, and mop out the kitchen.

—Marietta Holley, *Josiah Allen's Wife as a P.A. and P.I.*

THE "PREFAIS" to *My Opinions and Betsey Bobbet's* appeared in the Adams *Journal* in February 1873. A commentary under the headline "Literary Notices" in the 30 March issue praised the book as having "quaint pleasantry" and being "extremely readable." Even though her real name did not appear anywhere in the book, Marietta Holley could no longer maintain the remnant of literary anonymity. The news that she had written a book startled the neighborhood. To those nearby, she was the diminutive, taciturn, thirty-seven-year-old spinster who lived with her mother and queer sister on the Holley place. Although some folk knew that she had written a few stories and more poems, none had suspected that she was laboring on such an ambitious work. The publication announcement shattered the quiet of the women's household, rattling the neighborhood as well with an effect "something like a loud clap of thunder bursting forth from a teacup."[1]

Elisha Bliss had been right again in his assessment of what the book-buying public wanted. A notice at the end of the first year of publication claimed that not one book in five hundred published in the United States sold as well as hers already had, but it must be noted that the claim was made by a publisher, and as a group they were less than meticulous in their recordkeeping.[2] Still there is no doubt that sales were tremendous. Five editions had already appeared in the United States that year, and it was being published in London by Routledge and Sons as part of the Library of American Humor.

Portions of the book were appearing in the *Home Journal*. Many other fiction writers wrote serials for the inexpensive weeklies and better monthlies,[3] a strategy that Holley adopted and never abandoned. Consequently, the structure of her books, *Betsey Bobbet* included, is loosely episodic with characters introduced and reintroduced in succeeding segments. The work lacks the architecture of a novel. It is held together by the presence of Samantha and her place, even when she moves about on one of her "towers" (tours). Somehow, Samantha *is* a place. In a series of episodes taken from country life, local characters are introduced and developed, most notably members of Samantha's family and Betsey Bobbet. The novel chronicles the events that eddy around Samantha: quiltings, church meetings, visiting, and the Fourth of July in Jonesville. The book also describes Samantha's trip into New York City, where her country manners are set against the genteel sophistication of city folk. She meets Elizabeth Cady Stanton, Victoria Woodhull, Henry Ward Beecher, Susan B. Anthony, U. S. Grant, Schuyler Colfax, and Horace Greeley, and each encounter provides Samantha with an audience for her eloquence. The characters move around her, giving her an opportunity to lecture, sermonize, remonstrate, and practice "episodin' and allergorin'."

Those characters Holley created were very real to her. Holley, in an oblique admission that she was indeed Samantha, looked at the money accruing in her bank account and insisted that "certainly it is that Betsey Bobbet should have half of it."[4] From childhood Holley had known characters very much like the New Yorkers in *Betsey Bobbet*. In fact, there was a great flurry of speculation in the first years after the book appeared about precisely who had been the models for certain characters in the works—a sort of guessing game that caused considerable bad feelings and distrust of Holley. Growing up in the hinterland, she had had her relationships restricted to the immediate neighborhood where the qualities of one's kin and acquaintances were much discussed, analyzed, and criticized. People came to be known as individuals as well as types. Unlike their New England forebears, New Yorkers were somewhat more open to each other, more willing to share their feelings and problems. From the small set in church, school, and Hungerford's circle, Marietta had made enough study of character to create an assortment of folk to populate the fictional village of Jonesville.

Unlike Sarah Orne Jewett's Deephaven and Rose Terry Cooke's Bassett,[5] Holley's community cannot be readily identified as having particular geographical coordinates. Readers familiar with the topography and landmarks of New York State might have recognized enough descriptions and names to place Jonesville, but others simply accepted the setting as being some typical rural spot in the northeast. Like much of the women's fiction that preceded and followed it, Holley's work developed the controlling image of a restricted and structured space, within which—or in Samantha's case, outside of which—another, smaller space serves as its center.[6] The description of the Allen farm could be of a hundred small farms in the North Country, but it is also an accurate depiction of the Holley place as it appeared in 1873. The farmhouse was one-and-a-half stories, a cottage style; there was an orchard on the north side with a stream running through the hollow just beyond; the highway ran in front of the house, set off from the lawn by a fence; to the south stretched a great clover-filled meadow; and behind the house, on a flat terrace, was Samantha's magnificent garden.[7] Samantha and Josiah Allen live on their own farm outside of Jonesville on seventy-five acres that are paid for, thus establishing them as financially comfortable but still rural rather than village people. Samantha's interests extend beyond the narrow strip of farms that line the dusty road into Jonesville, however. In her preface, she echoes the same economic and social concerns that Holley herself had struggled with.

> In the first days of our married life, I strained nearly every nerve to help my companion Josiah along and take care of his children by his former consort, the subject of black African slavery also wearin' on me, and a mortgage of 200 and 50 dollars on the farm. But as we prospered and the mortgage was cleared, and the children were off to school, the black African also bein' liberated about the same time of the mortgage, then my mind bein' free from these cares—the great subject of Wimmen's Rites kept a goarin' me, and a voice kept a sayin' inside of me, "Josiah Allen's Wife, write a book givin' your views on the great subject of Wimmen's Rites."[8]

The custom of the humorous writers of the prewar era was to be coy in their prefaces about why they were putting out a book, disclaiming any self-interest. After the war they were more like Petroleum V. Nasby, likely to preface an edition with a statement about its merits and the author's altruistic purposes in letting the work appear before the public.[9] Holley took both conventions and twisted them to suit her central character's ethics and her own. Holley admits that her motive is to express her opinions, while Samantha insists that the mere statement of them in itself is significant: not that they will change anyone else's opinions, but that some things simply must be said whether anyone wants to hear them or not. As for many of the women Holley admired, farm and family came first of necessity, but Truth and Right were pressing to be articulated.

The truth was a Christian feminist's view of the rights that women and all people ought to have. The Civil War had diverted women's energies from the cause of woman's rights, and when it was ended, there was a division within the ranks of feminists: the radicals and the moderates each formed their own factions. Holley's (and Samantha's) ideas followed the prevailing moderate feminist thought of the 1870's. First women must have the right to vote. Without it they could not redress the wrongs committed by the liquor interests and errant politicians who were responsible for most of the evils of society. Recognition as voting citizens would permit women to bring about other needed reforms. Industrious and able girls would be afforded equal education and opportunities for work with equitable pay. They would be admitted to the professions, including law and the ministry. The structure of government in both church and state could remain substantially the same, as far as Holley was concerned, but with women at the polls and in office as well as wielding the power of their own money and property, the country—indeed the world—would soon be set to rights. The impact would shake every household. Girls would learn to value themselves as persons with talents and capabilities, which would set them free from the need to marry to achieve identity and security. With this freedom to choose marriage or not, they could avoid the abomination of divorce. They could cast off as well the bondage of conventional dress and free themselves to work, play, create, and breathe with full vitality. Without their hobbles, women would achieve partnership with men so that marriages, and the children they produced, could be healthy and happy, without the taint of servitude. The awful sentimentality of the genteel tradition would be replaced by authentic affection in relationships and activism in politics. It was a shining dream, but one that Holley and Samantha believed could be realized.

Holley's creation of Samantha as spokeswoman for these truths was prudent. Samantha is a married woman liable to the insults and precarious stature that the laws of the time allowed. Although she makes it clear that she and Josiah love one another and that he would do nothing to hurt her, she shows through the trials of her wedded female friends how the institution of marriage can enslave and belittle a woman by denying her any control over her property, her children, or her own body. Ironically Samantha dominates the relationship between wife and husband in her household, which was a condition that made her a heroine to women readers. To many men she was the comic domineering woman, but her sympathetic treatment of the foolish Josiah tempered their disdain for the type and made her an endearing character. With her humor directed at the foolishness and pretensions of both sexes, she won her audience's affection. In the quirky rhetoric of a country wife, and with great good humor, Samantha could draw analogies and negotiate arguments that shook the reader with laughter while they tweaked the conscience with recognition of one's own sexist sentiments. In her two-pronged attack on the double standard and the failings of both sexes, she took a position that gained her a reputation for tolerance and fair-mindedness. Part of her appeal lay in her criticism of the radical feminists of the time; her conservatism and pragmatism based on a sense of justice and expediency won audiences that would otherwise be antagonistic to her feminist ideals. At the same time Samantha's ardent nativism appealed to a populace struggling with its sense of self after the divisiveness of the Civil War. Her shrewdness and common sense were invincible in any argument, frequently leaving Josiah to stomp off to finish some chore rather than face the irrefutable logic in Samantha's wisdom. Always alert to ways to enhance women's reputations, she was quick to note their domestic, commercial, political, and artistic accomplishments. Her hardy self-confidence, independence, and intellectual vigor belied the prevailing notion that women were weak, passive, mindless, and powerless.

Samantha's feminism never weakened or shifted. From the beginning she espoused the rights of women to full humanity and citizenship. In diverse novels she focused attention on some issues more sharply than on others, such as chauvinism in the church, the evils of intemperance, the anguish of the race problem, but in all she championed the fundamental right of every person to be a whole person, and she did so with the disarming wit and apparent artlessness she displayed in the first book, *My Opinions and Betsey Bobbet's*.

Samantha receives little encouragement from Josiah. He insists that he will not hire anyone to read her book once it is written. With steadfast principle, Samantha begins the book anyway, the saga of Samantha Smith Allen and the family and friends that was to fill

"Samantha Advisin' President Grant." Illustration by True Williams for Marietta Holley, *Josiah Allen's Wife as a P.A. and P.I.* (Hartford, Ct., 1887), p. 400.

twenty-one novels and uncounted short stories during the next forty years. In the opening chapter, Samantha introduces her spouse Josiah, a widower with two children, Thomas Jefferson and Tirzah Ann. As Holley frequently did, Samantha ruminates a good deal on love and marriage, often questioning what love is and wondering why she married Josiah. It is a question she continues to ask herself even through the last of the Samantha books after she and Josiah have spent a lifetime together. At the beginning of this first installment in the serial adventures of the family, Samantha has been married to her "lawful pardner" for about fourteen years. From that perspective, she looks back on their courting with a mixture of wonder and resignation.

> I laughed at the idea of love in my blindness of eye. But the first time I sot my grey eye onto Josiah Allen I knew my fate . . . I married Josiah Allen . . . from pure love. Though why I loved him, I know not.[10]

Considering the chances she had had as a marriageable young woman, Samantha recollects that she rejected "offers from men, handsomer than him, with more intelect than him, with more riches than him, with less children than him. Why didn't I love these various men?"[11] It was a question Holley might have asked. Love remains a mystery for Samantha as it did for Marietta herself.

Josiah hardly seems a suitable object for such passion. Perhaps Holley remembered the nearby farmer whose wife had died leaving him with a dairy and children to care for, the widower whom Marietta's neighbor had suggested as a potential husband. This widower Josiah is a mite of a man, weighing only a hundred pounds, bearded and bald, with ideas that match his negligible weight. Samantha weighs 204 pounds, thereby outdoing him in heft as well as common sense and spiritual ballast. In spite of seeing his obvious failings, Samantha makes the ultimate commitment to Josiah, surrendering (temporarily) to him as her "fate," and she abides with him in "the purest and tenderest" of love. But Samantha's descriptions of love are not the stuff of the sentimental novels: not a kiss, a swoon, a flutter, but the beacon of the subtitle, "a pure light, though it has sputtered some, and in tryin' times such as washin' days and cleanin' house times has burnt down pretty low,—has never gone out."[12] The love between Samantha and Josiah is a kind, enduring, but platonic one. In fact, there is an obvious absence of sensuality or carnality in all of Samantha and Josiah's exchanges. About the only time they touch is when he holds her hand to take their marriage vows, or helps her down from a buggy, although she even prefers to do that unassisted. They exchange admiring glances as well as barbed retorts. Their regard for each other is constant, but they never share the physical closeness that Samantha conjures up for other characters. The children in Samantha's house are the product of a previous union for Josiah. Holley could only conceive of surrogate motherhood for her fictional ego. The presence of children in Samantha's life is accounted for in the only way Holley could imagine for Samantha and herself—as a kind of adoption.

Josiah Allen. Illustration by Frederick Opper for Marietta Holley, *Samantha at Saratoga* (Philadelphia, 1887), p. 42.

Thomas Jefferson and Tirzah Ann are nonetheless beloved by their stepmother even though she knows their faults. She laughs at their adolescent foibles, punctures their pretensions, nurses them, advises them, and loves them, though not equally. Without guilt, perhaps because she sees them as persons rather than as her own children, she can admit that Thomas Jefferson is her favorite, while Tirzah Ann is Josiah's. That may seem to have been an author's error in aligning sympathies, especially for a feminist, but Samantha's creed dictated that women are no better than men, only different, and that they are to be loved or hated according to their character, not their gender. That was a very moderate feminism, a pragmatic approach to the question of superiority and inferiority that earlier suffragists had contested.[13] Samantha set out to raise her stepchildren by her beliefs, admitting that "step-mothers have a pretty hard row to hoe"[14] but determined to do the duty nearest her. That included helping the seventeen-year-old boy see his folly and worrying aloud about Tirzah Ann's primary failing: sentimentality. Boys and girls were different, but only biologically. Otherwise they were both prone to the same foolishness and wrongheaded nonsense.

Samantha often insists that Josiah is like the general run of men: vain, impulsive, prone to bombast, and likely to be unfaithful if not closely watched. Furthermore, Samantha subscribes to the notion that most men—Josiah in particular—are primarily interested in two things: the well-being of their stomachs and maintenance of the status quo of patriarchal privilege. Not that Samantha thinks women are so superior. Many of the females that pass in and out of her life are similarly foolish, backward, and laughable, most notably the frantic spinster Betsey Bobbet. In creating the character of Betsey, Holley had refused to follow the advice of moderates such as Catharine Beecher to "do good by stealth" and "move in curves."[15] Her attack on the prevailing conceptions of biological destiny, women's economic productivity, and their legal franchise was open and direct. It was a clear contest between the forward-looking Samanthas and regressive Betsey Bobbets. After the Civil War women were "suffering from want of heroines." They needed new role models to heal the lost innocence of the wounds that the nation had suffered. Women writers needed to generate heroines like the ones they remembered from the antebellum age who were healthier, stronger, and more passionate in their convictions.[16]

As they did, Holley retained the memory of a generation of female pioneers. Women in the North Country were still intimidated by very real threats to their happiness, health, and security. The Civil War had taken most of the best men from the land. Some returned, but many were maimed in both visible and unseen ways. The women were left with the tasks of maintaining families, homesteads, and businesses. The distances between farms and settlements left them isolated from one another, unable to unburden themselves to a sister or friend. Frustration, repression, sickness, and fear haunted the women and girls. The number of suicides among them in the twenty years after 1855 is painful testimony to the futility they felt. Brides hung themselves in their in-laws' attics; mothers drowned their baby daughters and then themselves in farm ponds; old women with unnamed illnesses drank lethal doses of laudanum. The panthers that were still seen in Giddingsville and the black bears that fished the creek in Pierrepont Manor were at least targets that the women could shoot at. The despair of unpaid mortgages, plaguing sickness, and marriages without love were dangers which only death could protect them from. Out of the struggle to survive came Holley's vision of the country wife as heroine.

With a stroke of faith bolstered by her pride in her "foremothers," Holley created the stalwart Samantha. But the character needed a foil. The skinny spinster Betsey Bobbet provides one in ways that Josiah cannot. Betsey's single aim in life is to be some man's wife. Even the verses that she writes for the Jonesville newspapers the *Gim-*

"I LOVE THAT OLD MAN, AND WISH HIM AWFUL WELL."

Samantha and Uncle Sam. Illustrated by Baron C. deGrimm for Marietta Holley, *Samantha at the World's Fair* (New York, 1890), p. 65.

let and the *Auger* are pathetic attempts to announce to any man who can read that she is available, just waiting to become the clinging vine to his sturdy oak. She is opposed to any "wimmen's rights" except the right to marry, especially when there's a man within earshot. Precisely why she wants to marry is made very clear: she craves the status conferred by the title of wife. She may also have desired companionship, but certainly not passion. Spinsters in literature had typically been prudes, supposedly repressing any lust that they might have felt. Widows, on the other hand, had the reputation of being sexually interesting, though many of them in literature and life chose not to remarry. They often enjoyed some economic freedom, the wife's status without the strain, and a certain social influence.[17] Clearly, Betsey could be a more effective antifeminist character as a pining spinster rather than as a widow.

Samantha describes the maiden Betsey with characteristic kindness and candor: "Betsey haint handsome."[18] As a matter of fact, she is the typical ugly spinster—spindly, with tiny eyes, less hair than she once had, a big nose, and false teeth. Besides her physical defects, she lacks faculty, "a kind of dazzling skill in feminine and household affairs equivalent to brilliant satiric wit in conversation,"[19] and she cannot even cook. Samantha maintains that Betsey's worst difficulty is her awful sentimentalism, which is most obvious in her affected speech and pretensions to gentility. Betsey chases after every man who might be eligible, often disregarding his suitability as a mate. She will go so far as to visit a man whose wife is dreadfully ill, bringing the conversation around to what his needs might be should the wife succumb. When she finally does snare a spouse, it is old Simon Slimpsey, a widower with a passel of children. Having heard that he and seven or eight of his children were sick, she volunteers to care for them, moving in under his very roof. In his weakened condition, Betsey has her way with him; they are wed. Betsey Bobbet Slimpsey's story continues through the remaining narratives, however, finally ending with a poem in which Betsey, worn out, wishes that she were a widow. In the poem "I Wish I Was a Widder," as it appears in the *Gimlet*, Betsey envisions widowhood:

> The warfare past, the horrors done,
> With maiden ease and pride of wife,
> The dignity of wedded one,
> The calm and peace of single life;
> Oh strangely sweet this lot doth seem,
> A female widder is my theme.[20]

In spite of her trials in the married state and the influence of Samantha, Betsey remains unconverted to the cause of female selfhood. Even seeking release from the bonds of matrimony, she defines herself as the "relict" of a man.

The relationship between Betsey and Marietta Holley is hardly complex. Holley ironically projects two of her own qualities onto Betsey: spinsterhood and "poetness." In the process she wrenches those conditions until they become parodies of her own blessed singleness and artistic endeavor, thereby posing her fear of being reduced to those grotesque positions. Although Betsey and Holley are opposites, Samantha and Marietta are in many ways the same woman, or halves of Holley's self. Aside from their weights, they resemble each other. Samantha's grey eyes, like Holley's brown ones, are deep and magnetic, and her nose is an "honorable Roman" one. Samantha is the woman Marietta might have been if she had not been gifted with her writing and cursed with her shyness. Samantha Allen is unreservedly a down-home character, content with her country manners, values, and neighbors. Marietta Holley aspired to gentility, travel with a better class of folk, and a gracious life. Samantha is assertive and garrulous. Marietta was diffident and taciturn.

Both the writer and her persona were ardent feminists and nativists, and both supported the concept of Christian fellowship over restrictive church membership. Samantha is a member of the Methodist Episcopal church; Marietta's allegiance was to the Baptist church. In Adams, however, the two churches were closely linked by friendships across both congregations and a blurring of devotional practice. The ministers of the two churches occasionally exchanged pulpits. Most of the distinctions made were focused on the issue of baptism, specifically the question of immersion. One of Marietta's favorite stories was about the little girl who wanted to baptize her three cats. The first one was thrust under water and came up sputtering. The second was reluctant but received the same sacrament. The third and largest cat fought until the child gave up saying, "All right, then, *be* a Methodist!"[21] The child's concern with religious doctrine is significant. Both Marietta and Samantha practiced the newly feminized religion prevailing in the East. Women had long since taken over the responsibilities for the Sabbath schools, adding those duties to those of church housekeeping. Children were being brought into the church earlier, in part as a consequence of the new sense that the human spirit was somehow born ready for salvation. At the same time the Calvinist image of God as the stern, wrathful male figure was giving way to the form of a very personal, loving, gentle parent.[22] The notion of infant damnation was past at midcentury,[23] and after the Civil War children were seen as the way of redemption for American society, particularly to Samantha and Marietta.

The hope for that society was invested in children, free-thinking women, and certain great men such as Henry Ward Beecher. He is revered by Samantha as he was by Holley, although Josiah Allen's wife discusses his merit in her own homely rhetoric.

> But not once in 100 years does Nature turn out such a man as H.W.B. It takes her longer than that to get her ingregiences and materials together to make such a pure sweet nature, such a broad charity, and such a intellect as hisen. Why, if the question had been put to me before I was born, whether I would be born his sister or the twin sister of the queen of England, I'd never give a second thought. . . . For he is a king not made by the layin' on of earthly hands, he is God's own annointed, and that is royalty that can't be upsot.[24]

The optimism that both Marietta and Samantha felt was the consequence of their religion and pragmatic feminism. Samantha contentedly practices hers in the relative comfort of her rural home. Marietta's early poverty had marked her, made her see how women were economically dependent and how that dependence shaped their identities. It was an awareness that drove Marietta to want more than the minimal creature comforts that Samantha enjoyed.

Samantha favored the simple dress and apron of the country wife, while Marietta had her clothes made for her by seamstresses in Adams or New York City. Marietta was bustled and curved at the waist, though a male journalist who visited her commented that her skirts were not so tightly hobbled as fashion dictated. Marietta and Samantha were both as concerned with dress reform as with legal reform to liberate women. Twenty years earlier Amelia Bloomer had begun a campaign against the laced and bustled dress that women were expected to wear by adopting an ensemble consisting of a belted tunic over a short skirt and loose, ankle-length pantaloons. Elizabeth Cady Stanton, Susan B. Anthony, and others followed suit. Dr. Mary Walker, an army surgeon in the Civil War, had stopped wearing skirts and had begun to dress in full trousers under a long coat, keeping her hair in curls, however, so there might be no confusion about her gender. Holley recognized the need for loose, comfortable clothing that eased work and permitted healthful exercise, but she—like the more moderate feminists before her—knew that focusing attention on such radical changes diverted energy from more pressing, basic issues. The writer had reacted with respect but not approval when Dr. Walker visited for several days at Adams in December 1871. Although she did not lecture, she was highly visible. Wearing the pantaloons that she advocated, she aroused the public comment that "everyone was surprised at her agreeable looks and manner in spite of her dress, admittedly healthy."[25] Holley's interest in women's well-being went further than Dr. Walker's and Amelia Bloomer's attire, however. In November 1872, while Marietta was working on revisions of *Betsey Bobbet*, a Dr. Everett, a married woman physician, had lectured to a small audience in Adams on women's health practices, exciting some controversy. What she said is lost, but the following week letters of support for her radical ideas for female health appeared in the local paper.[26] Holley incorporated these experiences into Samantha's. On her trip to New York City, Samantha met Dr. Walker. Bewildered by the look of her apparel, even confused about Walker's gender, Samantha nevertheless respected the issue that the feminist doctor was addressing. However, she made it clear the pantaloons deviate from her "megumness and moderation" as much as whalebone corsets do.

At the time there was an epidemic of poor health among American middle- and upper-class women, many of whom were ill with neurasthenic ailments as well as the physical complications of childbirth, the scourge of tuberculosis, "green-sickness," and a host of other diseases. The lower classes were similarly afflicted, even though they had no leisure for illness: they worked until they died.[27] Marietta's early awareness of her own health, reinforced by the consciousness of sickness and death around her, led her to advocate simplicity and comfort in dress, not just for modesty but for health. Like Samantha, she kept to a regimen of wholesome, simple foods, fresh air, rest, and moderate exercise. The function of the routine was more than precautionary for Marietta. It was at once a luxury and a concession to her work ethic.

Suffering from fear of the dark and insomnia, she slept poorly if at all. Mornings she would rise at seven and eat her favorite breakfast, a meal fit for Samantha: four pancakes, creamed potatoes, four stewed prunes, a pot of coffee, a pitcher of Jersey cream, Jersey butter, and a piece of homemade sausage. Not trusting sausage from a market—the way others did not dare buy clothes made in urban garment districts because of the diseases they might carry—Marietta had her beef and pork specially ground and seasoned with sage grown in her own garden, salt, pepper, and a smidgen of sugar. Soon after the success of her first book, Holley began using her mornings for writing, sometimes staying in her room upstairs until dinnertime, when she would join her mother, sister, and the farmhands for a hearty midday meal. Immediately after the clutter of the meal was cleared, Marietta and Sylphina retired for a nap. Even when the writer's fame lured carriage loads of visitors to her home, she insisted that she would have her nap undisturbed even if the king and queen should call.[28] Afternoons were spent in the garden, henhouse, or barn. The family had little livestock, usually a sow, the pony, Marietta's hens, and a couple of milk cows. The farm chores were finished after a light supper. Before going up to bed for the night, Marietta ate a one-inch cube of local cheese, believing that it was good for her digestion. Years later she attributed her long life to that habit.[29] During this period, she was healthy and happy beyond her expectations, in part because she saw her future expanding. She had a literary career at last.

The success of *My Opinions and Betsey Bobbet's* is astonishing when one considers that the woman suffrage movement engaged only a very few men and women. At the height of its power and visibility in the nineteenth century, the movement "had the active support of less than 10% of the women in the United States."[30] If it was not the argument that won her readers, it may have been the good-humored vision of rural life with its quirky characters and quaint customs and manners. The novel is textured with the events that knit together daily farm and small-town life. There are surprise parties when crowds of friends arrive unexpectedly to make a potluck supper, quilting parties, courtings, weddings, funerals, peddlers and gypsies passing through, donation parties, and harvest suppers. Although the catalogue of women's chores is included, there is little mention of the brutalizing labor of country life or the endurance that was required to transcend it.

Publishers began to seek Holley's fiction for their magazines, knowing that her name would sell an issue. *Peterson's* published five of her stories in 1875. Because one of the stories appeared in two parts, half of *Peterson's* issues that year contained prose fiction by Marietta Holley. All five stories were in the sentimental style rather than in Samantha's dialect. Holley felt that it was more appropriate to a magazine such as *Peterson's* and suited the works of the popular women writers such as Frances Hodgson Burnett and Ella Wheeler, whose works appeared in the same issues.[31]

Both Holley and Samantha Allen were gaining reputations among the writers and publishers who were busily making money in the popular market. But that market was based in New York City and Philadelphia, while Marietta remained at home in distant northern New York State.

The literati of New Hartford and New York City may have thought that Holley's bucolic life was boring or socially barren, but at this period the shy woman found the confines of her rural retreat satisfying. She remained at home because she chose to stay close to her loving mother, the maternal center and the known. Holley often said that she was afraid to travel anywhere alone, even into heaven. For her, the red cottage was a haven that allowed her to range far in her spiritual and aesthetic pursuits. In a revision of the poem that she sent to Longfellow, "Isabelle and I," which appeared in the winter of 1875, she describes the wealth and splendor that surrounds Isabelle, who travels in a glittering swirl. The speaker of the poem, clearly Marietta, has a cottage instead of a mansion, peace of mind and—most important—imagination. She concludes:

Why should I envy Isabelle
When thus so easily,
Upon a tropic flower's perfume
I float across the sea.[32]

In this very Emersonian mood she refused to travel, believing that in idle tourism one "carries ruins to ruins." Although she always delighted in a visit from a friend, she was fond of quoting Emerson in defense of her reluctance to repay those visits: "To my friend I write a letter, and from him receive a letter. . . . It suffices me. In these warm lines the heart will trust itself, as it will not to the tongue."[33] Paying visits was a rash, silly act that increased the self-importance of the visitor, who would assume that the hostess wanted the company. It was a custom Marietta always avoided, although Samantha was a great one for bustling in to visit on a whim, secure that whether she was expected or not, her call would be worthwhile to visitor and host.

The only visitor whom Holley herself welcomed unreservedly was Bliss. He had asked her to write a book about Samantha and Josiah visiting the centennial exposition at Philadelphia. By March 1876 an agreement had been made that she would do so, but she refused to attend the centennial herself. In May Bliss visited her again at her home presumably to bring her brochures, maps, photos, and travel material to aid her in her description of what the Allens would see on their "tower." At the same time Holley was invited to use her poet's skill to write a centennial hymn to be sung at the academy of music in Philadelphia on 12 June, a hymn composed to be sung to "some sacred old air already embalmed in the heart of the nation."[34]

With the Emancipation Proclamation enacted, and her book on woman's rights written, Holley had a new opportunity in the writing of a book about the centennial to hold forth on another of her fiercely held convictions: temperance. Under the Local Option Law, the town of Adams had gone "no license" in 1875, while Ellisburgh, the township in which Holley actually resided, allowed licensing. Clearly the abuse of alcohol was an issue which Holley felt strongly about. Much of *Samantha at the Centennial* concerns temperance in its various degrees of fervor: the temperates who believed alcohol could be used without abuse and for medical reasons; the moderates who would ban whiskey but allow wine and beer; and the total abstinence people, or teetotalers, who would allow no drinks with any alcohol content and were recognized by the *T*s on their pledge cards. Although the evil of John Barleycorn had been touched on in *My Opinions and Betsey Bobbet's*, Samantha's next book attacked the issue head-on.

Everything seemed to be going well for Marietta. The family had come through the terrible winter of 1875 quite well, and although Marietta was very ill in the spring, she recovered in the warm summer air. Age, fatigue, and illness seemed the only things that threatened the three women, and these they guarded against as best they could. An aura of peace and seclusion surrounded them until the autumn. One November morning the women woke to discover that the barn had been broken into. The only item missing was the sorrel pony's harness, but there was evidence that the thief had intended to steal the pony and buggy too if he had not been frightened off.[35] The harness was replaceable, but the peace of mind that Holley was enjoying began to suffer irreparable shocks. Henhouses were being raided at night. The newspaper published a line warning that the gypsies were on the road again moving through the county. Marietta was struggling to finish the book that Bliss had commissioned, working through the winter of 1876 and the spring of 1877. She said that she had put everything she knew into *My Opinions and Betsey Bobbet's*, so the second work was more like hack journalism for her. In the autumn of 1877, with the manuscript nearly finished, Marietta was alarmed at her mother's being stricken with pneumonia. With winter approaching, such an illness was especially threatening. When the doctor told Marietta that the chances for her mother's recovery were slight, Marietta herself fell ill and took to her bed.

The loss of her mother was the greatest woe she could imagine. For a while Mary rallied, and Marietta recovered her own health and composure. She finished the centennial book. Then in the morning hours of the first Monday in November, Mary died of the pneumonia from which she had not truly recovered. On Wednesday, Marietta, Sylphina, and the close family conducted her funeral in the best room of the farm cottage. As John Milton Holley had been, Mary Taber Holley was buried in the family plot in the cemetery adjoining the Episcopal Church in Pierrepont Manor.[36]

Within two weeks Holley's new book was out, again without Holley's name appearing anywhere in it: *Josiah Allen's Wife as a P.A.* [Promiscuous Advisor] *and P.I.* [Private Investigator]: *Samantha at the Centennial.* Mark Twain declared that the work was "brilliant, a grand improvement on the first."[37] It was illustrated with the wry drawings of True Williams, one of Twain's illustrators. Like Holley, Williams was from the North Country, although he could not have been a farm boy. In one illustration he shows a man milking a cow while seated on the wrong side of the animal. The mistake caused great merriment for readers, the author, and Williams. Holley admired his artwork and believed in his genius, but his drinking to excess prevented their being better friends. Drink made him disgusting to her. It prevented him from realizing his potential, which Holley saw as a crime. For her Williams was a splendid symbol of what the abuse of alcohol did: it dulled creativity, subverted one's God-given gifts, and made victims of one's family. When he was sober, Williams was a welcome visitor, but otherwise Marietta sent him off to his relatives in Watertown to dry out. She mocked his dependency, recalling how Bliss had had to shut Williams away with a manuscript in order to get him to finish it before the drinking took him over. When Williams visited Marietta's home with his young wife, Marietta took the opportunity to lecture him on his duty to abandon Demon Drink for the woman's sake. After one such sermon, Williams left and never returned,[38] although he continued to write her fancifully decorated letters full of advice and offers to illustrate other of her books.

With the popularity of Williams' illustrations, the interest in America's birthday, and the success of her previous book, *Samantha at the Centennial* was destined to sell well. As usual, the first third or so of the narrative is concerned with getting the Allen family organized. Squabbles have to be settled, illnesses accommodated, travel plans cussed and discussed. Thomas Jefferson and Tirzah Ann are more active characters in this book, having grown into willful young adults with love lives and futures of their own. Thomas Jefferson has become quite a student, eventually to be a lawyer (or doctor, depending upon which novel one reads). Samantha claims that it is through his reading to her that she knows the classics as well as she knows

Foxe's Book of Martyrs and the Bible. The second novel abounds in literary references and paraphrases. Everyone from Milton to Shakespeare and Ruskin is mentioned. It was frequently said by Holley's friends (and a few detractors) that she always had a book in her hand. Her personal library was disposed of at her death, but it seems obvious from the allusions, as well as the fractured paraphrases and quotations, that Holley read most of the literature that was considered to be the requisite for a sound education. There are echoes of Carlyle, Plato, Tennyson, and some of the American poets, although there are none of fiction writers. As though to chide the learned gentlefolk who spouted their little Latin and less Greek to make themselves seem better than most, Samantha drops a bit of learning into the midst of an episode to demonstrate that the masterpieces have merit not because they are intrinsically valuable, but because they illustrate some subtle truth about real human experience. For example, when Samantha tartly admonishes an Adventist about shirking her earthly work, she paraphrases Carlyle: "I have always believed in layin' holt of the duty next to you, and doin' *some* things, things He has commanded."[39] Mixing learned language and homely rhetoric was a useful strategy for the farm girl who grew up coveting booklearning. When she acquired it, it was clear to her that literature reflected experience, not created it. Before she began her program of study through reading, she had been steeped in the torture, sacrifice, and executions of the Protestant martyrs as they were detailed in the illustrated *Foxe's Book of Martyrs*, which was on every Sunday school shelf. Holley often has Samantha refer to the work, particularly to compare her own sufferings to those of the Christian reformers. Although the book made an enormous impression on the girl who was wrestling with her own salvation, it was not the reading matter Holley herself claimed as being most significant to her. That distinction was shared by Emerson's writings and the Bible.[40]

Marietta's solitary ways had kept her out of the main current of literary and political events. As the popularity of her books increased, well-known people came to make her acquaintance or pay homage. Some became friends. In January 1878 Will Carleton was giving a reading in Adams.[41] His best-selling book of 1873, *Farm Ballads*, had endeared him to audiences that relished gentle rustic humor and a celebration of rural life. After his evening's entertainment, he met Holley at the home of her cousin the hotelkeeper in Adams. A long, warm conversation developed, during which he gave Holley the impression that he knew her books and stories better than she herself did. There was a mingling of admiration and envy in his feelings for her, and a great deal of sincere affection. He had even named his paper in Jonesville, Ohio, after one of Holley's fictitious small-town papers. Carleton and Holley had talked late into the evening when he asked her to stay over at her cousin's so that they might continue their acquaintance.[42] She refused, although she probably did not tell him that it was because she feared sleeping away from home. Soon after he left Adams to continue his speaking circuit, they began to correspond. His letters were bright, casual, concerned with the business of writing and publishing, often trying to make appointments or inquire after her health or pass on a bit of gossip. Their friendship was nourished by many things, not the least being a sense that she with her Samantha stories and he with his *Farm Ballads* were singing elegiac hymns to America's rural purity.

Others of her friendships were based in a shared political ethic. Susan B. Anthony had been addressing assemblies around the East when finally she arrived at the Cooper Opera House to lecture in September 1880. Admission was either twenty-five or thirty-five cents to hear and see the suffragist deliver her lecture "Woman Wants Bread, Not the Ballot."[43] Two years before Holley had received a letter from Anthony inviting her to write something for the suffragist paper the *National Citizen.* The letter ironically bears the saluation "My Dear Miss Betsey Bobbitt," even though eventually most of Holley's friends came to call her Samantha.

Anthony's letter was a response to the first two Samantha books. Enclosed were congressional committee reports against the Sixteenth Amendment petitions with her suggestion that "Samantha may have a comment to make on it." She urged Holley to send them "any of the things *too good*—that is *too decidedly* woman suffrage for the popular press." She included a list of the women who were going to attend the thirtieth-anniversary celebration of the movement: Lucretia Mott, Elizabeth Cady Stanton, Matilda Joslyn Gage, Sojourner Truth, and so on. Anthony pleaded with Holley: "Come—in cog. [*sic*] if you choose—only be here—. . . . But if you cannot be present, will you not send a letter to be read and printed—that we may have the influence of your name as well as good word—."[44] Holley did not attend the celebration, preferring not to travel or be put in a position where she might be asked to speak. However, when Anthony was in Adams, Holley took the opportunity to meet her. They spent a brief but pleasant time in Anthony's hotel room after the lecture. In *My Opinions and Betsey Bobbet's* Holley had written a scene describing a meeting between Samantha and Susan B. Anthony. Samantha described the latter as "smart and sensible lookin', but she was some like me, she wont never be hung for her beauty." The two discuss their commitment to the women's movement, Anthony saying she had married the cause, while Samantha admits she might have if she had not married Josiah first. Maybe Susan B. Anthony and Marietta Holley discussed that fictional scene and their real differences that night in Adams. Afterwards Anthony compared Holley to another friend and feminist: "You are like Elizabeth Cady Stanton. I often tell her she is as bold as a lion in her own chimney corner."[45] Anthony's appreciation for Holley's work persisted, and she respected Holley's reluctance to speak out in person. She continued to send the writer data and suggestions—as well as invitations—but the two women never met one another again.

Anthony's was not the only invitation to appear or speak at a convention that Holley refused. Because of her stances on "wimmen's rights," temperance, and corruption in government, she was often asked to speak on those matters. As early as 1877 a letter from Frances E. Willard invited Holley to be a delegate to the annual convention of the Women's National Christian Temperance Union in Chicago. Only three years earlier Willard had become president of that group; by 1879 she would be president of the National WCTU, bringing an energy and shrewdness that would make it the largest women's group in the country. She recognized the link between the impulse of the nation's women to protect their homes from the ravages of drink and its attendant vices and their inability to vote against liquor interests. Thus she tried to bring women to the suffrage cause through the temperance movement. Willard stressed the scope of the delegations: twenty-three states were represented; women of all Christian denominations, with marked abilities and influence, would attend. She included with the note a leaflet describing the aims of the organization. Thinking that she had anticipated all of Holley's possible objections, but knowing that the reclusive writer did not travel, she concluded: "Representing as you do so much of beneficient influence, it is earnestly hoped that you may accept the invitation hereby extended, to send us words of counsel or encouragement." It appears that Holley sent some response, perhaps a poem, but what was most important was that Willard's invitation began a correspondence that escalated over the next year. By 1879 Willard was signing her hurriedly scratched postcards "Sister Frances" and addressing her chatter to "My dear Samanthy."[46] The correspondence includes Willard's itineraries, requests for a photo, and snatches of what progress the WCTU was making. Even when Willard herself was not well enough to write, or too busy, she would ask Anna Gordon to do so. There were always plans for Willard and her associate Gordon to visit the farm. Willard, born in

New York State, was herself reared in the relative solitude of the frontier and, like Holley, had remained unmarried. They shared their rural roots as well as their commitment to suffrage and temperance, but Holley continued to give her support through Samantha rather than from the podium.

It seemed that everyone was reading or talking about the Samantha books. Betsey Bobbet clubs had been formed where friends met to read chapters form the books, sometimes taking parts to render dramatically. It was not just an idle woman's afternoon amusement. In Chicago one club included a senator and three Presbyterian clergymen.[47] Clara Barton sometimes joined, preferring to read the part of Betsey, but more often when she needed respite from her work establishing the Red Cross, she would spend a day sleeping and reading Samantha.[48] Several vocal ensembles became known as the Jonesville Choir, although the Adams Baptist Church choir was their prototype. It was busy meeting engagements at the Cooper Opera House at Adams and giving concerts in other towns. By the spring of 1880 Betsey Bobbet clubs were meeting and performing dramatic readings all around the state. The clubs used local talent and interpreted well-known episodes, so they were very well attended, but not by Holley. She was working on a new novel for the American Publishing Company, *My Warward Pardner or My Trials with Josiah, the Widow Bump and Etcetery*. Hoping to have the manuscript to Elisha Bliss in time for the book to come out for the Christmas season, she was writing intensively. At the same time, she had begun a new venture.

In March she had helped organize and fund a library in Adams. It was incorporated under the name The Holley Circulating Library Association with Marietta as vice-president.[49] In May the local Betsey Bobbet Club was scheduled to perform the play that had evolved from the informal presentations of the Allen family's vicissitudes. The profits were to benefit the proposed Holley Library, and Marietta had quietly announced that she would double the box office receipts. An amateur production titled *Betsey Bobbet* had already been presented in Buffalo, New York. Emma Babcock of Fredonia had seen it, made as good a copy of it as she could, and then sent the script to Holley who "revised it making such alterations as she thought best." The drama was a six-act production with bits of dialogue taken straight from the books. The night of the performance a typically fierce spring storm struck, but the hall was filled.[50] So great was the success that the little band of troupers was asked to repeat the performance in other towns and cities around the state, always playing to a full house. The summer passed happily for Marietta, and though she regretted that her mother was not with her to see the success, she believed that the spirits of those we love are always near us and took comfort in that. It was a productive period for Holley. She was happy with her work, her success, her publisher, and her new friends.

Then in October she received a telegram informing her that Elisha Bliss was dead. Within three years two persons she had depended upon were gone—her mother and Bliss. Bliss's son Frank immediately assumed his father's responsibilities. For Mark Twain, that was the end of his association with American Publishing Company. Marietta shifted her affection to Frank and maintained a certain allegiance to the firm that had first published her work, but the relationship with the younger Bliss was never that of mentor to writer as it had been with the elder. Fortunately, her work on *My Wayward Pardner* was finished. By November it was in the press, to be delivered around Christmastime by the local canvasser. In Holley's area, that was a young man named Will Shaver.

When the book appeared, the byline was Josiah Allen's Wife, but in parentheses beneath it, in type one quarter the size, was Marietta Holley. Samantha's voice is even stronger and clearer than before, with Holley more firmly in control of the tricks of verbal comedy. Furthermore, the book shows more skill in structure than the first two novels, using foreshadowing, smoother narrative development, and stronger character sketches. The essential conflict is over Josiah's lusting after the widow Bump—or Samantha's suspicion that he does. It is also an attack on many of the injustices to women that the woman suffrage movement had identified. One of the worst indignities is identified with the Mormon practice of polygamy, and Samantha, who suspects that Josiah is leaning toward the idea of converting, lashes out at it as a shameful sin. Feelings about Mormonism had been high in New York State since Joseph Smith's vision in Palmyra. By 1880 the Mormons were in Utah, but the intolerance that Holley and many of her contemporaries felt still simmered. Within a month of the publication of *My Wayward Pardner*, Holley's second work against Mormonism appeared.

The book-length poem *The Lament of the Mormon Wife* was also published by the American Publishing Company. Lavishly illustrated and printed on heavy gilt-edged paper, it was a labor of love. It was not only Holley's first poem so published, but it was on marriage, the subject she most often considered, and in this case her topic was a perversion of the sacrament that she still did not fully understand. The lament is spoken by the first wife of the four that the Mormon in her poem had married. She recounts their early love before he became a

Mormon. Their baby dies; he converts and marries other women with whom he has two healthy sons. The first wife, now older and barren, lives in an attic room, going to the servants' quarters for her "daily dole of bread and meat," hoping for death. Even recognizing the husband's sin, she still loves him, remembering that "he had an affectionate heart/Before he became a saint."[51]

Agitation over the rights and righteousness of Mormons had been abroad in the country for several years. Although "the Utah troubles" were considered from legal and moral perspectives, Marietta's interest in the issues seemed to be focused not on the doctrinal difficulties but on the position of women in a patriarchal, polygamous sect. In 1876 an exposé by an apostate wife of Brigham Young was published under the title *Wife Number Nineteen; or, The Story of A Life In Bondage*. It is not certain that Holley read the book, but when considering the problems with Mormonism, she turned inward again to examine the effect of plural marriage from a woman's perspective. The consequences of polygamy had come very close to her in the summer of 1870. There was a flurry of scandal in Pierrepont Manor when an itinerant Mormon preacher courted and won a buxom young widow. After a few months he told her to prepare to follow him west in a short time. When a few weeks passed and she had received no word, she wrote his brother. His reply revealed that her husband already had two wives with him in the West. No names were mentioned in the newspaper account of this little drama, but in a village the size of Pierrepont Manor, everyone would know the identity of the woman as well as the consequences of her Mormon marriage.[52] The images for the *Lament of the Mormon Wife* had been brewing in Holley's imagination for ten years when her poem finally appeared.

It was an impassioned work, but the lurching rhythm and wrenched rhymes were too contrived. The homespun wisdom of Samantha was winning Holley more friends and fame than the *Lament* would. In February 1881, *Betsey Bobbet* was being presented by thirty young ladies at Claverack College on the Hudson.[53] The president of the college, Dr. Alonzo Flack, had written Holley several admiring letters, declaring how much he enjoyed her works and inviting her to visit the college and be his family's guest. Claverack had grown from a seminary into a college where, beginning in 1869, a woman could earn a "mistress of arts" degree that was on a par with the "master of arts" degree. In addition to its aura of feminism, the college had strong links to the Methodist Conference, in which Flack was prominent.[54] Samantha's message suited him so well that he even read passages to the students during chapel. When all his invitations failed to lure her to

Claverack, he sent a telegram saying he would arrive that same day at her home. Upon arrival, he announced that he would take her back himself to Claverack. When she sputtered about how she could not possibly go because she was not ready, and it would take her two or three weeks to prepare for such a journey, he seated himself on the hall chair and declared that he would just wait. Holley reconsidered, faced with Flack's determination, and agreed to go with him. First she insisted that he stay a day to attend the commencement exercises at the Hungerford Collegiate Institute in Adams. Flack met Holley's friend General Hungerford and made a wager that, contrary to everything Hungerford knew about Holley's loathing of travel, she would go with him.[55]

The following morning Marietta made her first trip out of her limited circuit. It was July 1881. The time had come for her to leave the narrow precincts where she had spent all of her forty-five years, precisely half of her lifetime.

4

THE GREAT TOUR

Each soul has got to embark and sail out alone, out into the silence and the shadows—sail out into the mysterious Beyond.

We can't get away from ourselves, and get a real change, nohow, unless we knock our heads in and make idiots and lunys of ourselves. Movin' our bodies round here and there is only a shadow of change, a mockery.

—Marietta Holley, *My Wayward Pardner*

ALONZO FLACK'S PERSEVERANCE had finally nudged Holley out of the region where she had been born. He had made his appearance at a propitious time. The old orderly life for Marietta had changed. By the summer of 1881 she had truly come to terms with her mother's death. The narrow cottage that she and Finy shared was emptier, no longer the haven of maternal love that it had been. More and more, it was a responsibility unshared. In addition, a very large part of her life—as well as her duty—was gone, and the urge to see more of the country she loved so fiercely was great. Perhaps the others who had tried to lure her out of the county failed because they did not accommodate her dread of traveling anywhere alone. Dr. Flack, with his strong Methodist Conference affiliations and sterling reputation, seemed safe enough as a companion.

The trip by train to Hudson, where Mrs. Flack and several children met them, must have been a quiet one, for Marietta was not a voluble talker like Samantha. A good deal of her time, as usual, was spent looking about her, studying her companions as well as the countryside. When she arrived in Claverack, the Flacks took her into their grand home, making her comfortable beyond any dream she had or desire she expressed. The one- or two-day stay lengthened into a six-week sojourn.[1] Mrs. Flack arranged several brief excursions for herself and Marietta, occasionally including the Reverend Dr. Flack in their party. When the women went together alone, they used the hostess' own docile, steady horse and surrey, but when Flack joined them, they were driven in the larger carriage with a coachman taking direction from Flack. Holley was given the seat of honor beside him, and she seemed to revel in the dizzying rides down the hillsides so long as Dr. Flack was in control. Only with him would she dare to have the reins let out and the horses given their heads while she was tossed about against him on the seat.[2] The Flacks took the mountain routes to show off the Catskills which were an awesome contrast to the hills and hollows of Jefferson County. They stayed at small resorts, met local celebrities, and attended special church services and sermons as far away as the Berkshires. Holley devoured the lore of the rural areas, visiting old fenced graveyards to touch the lichened stones of settlers with resonant Dutch names that sounded so different to her ear from the jumble of English names in the North Country.

It was during this visit along the Hudson River that Holley recorded her first experience with what she called "the unexplained." She was still occupied somewhat with the specter of death, fascinated with dead daughters and ruins and monuments to money that could not buy longevity. In great detail she spoke of finding one particular gravestone: a bas-relief image of a man with a large tear on his cheek had beneath it his dead wife's name, and underneath it all, the motto Reconciled. It was emblematic of this period in Holley's life. Still, the seed of spiritualist belief that the young schoolmistress had dropped so many years before had taken root. Marietta was beginning to notice small events and odd coincidences, phenomena that she might explain as communications from the other side of death.

One trip with her hosts to hear Dr. Flack deliver a sermon required that they make the twelve-mile return trip at night by carriage. It was a moonlit summer night along the Hudson. Suddenly the horses reared in terror. Even when the two men attempted to calm them, the horses refused to go forward on that road until a considerable time had passed. The chances are that there was a sound natural explanation for the event, a wild animal at the roadside, perhaps, but Marietta accepted it as a sign of some sort, and it both deepened her interest in spiritualism and increased her fear of horses. Holley suggested that it was not animals but spirits that were about that night.

Having shown her the regional landmarks and made her feel quite at home, Mrs. Flack persuaded Holley to go to New York City. They went by train to pick up the steamer *Albany*, and then to the city, Holley having overcome her fear of water enough to make the short trip. This visit to New York City was a brief one, but it was rich with glamor and sophistication: galleries, immense churches, finely appointed hotels, and lavish apartments. It was a feast for Marietta, especially when she was introduced into the society of important clergy and statesmen who would later supply her with documents, contacts, and insights for her work. Although she would never have the camaraderie of a literary coterie such as those that nourished other writers, this new group of friends who were undemanding and uncritical made it possible for her to reach out to the world even after she had returned to her provincial home. The leaders of this new set were the Reverend and Mrs. John P. Newman. Not yet a bishop, Newman was preaching at a Methodist church on Fifth Avenue.[3] The friendship between the Flacks and Newmans had begun when the women were schoolmates.[4] Mrs. Newman immediately embraced Holley, sweeping her into their circle of friends. She offered to lend the two women the Newmans' own house because they were leaving for a trip themselves the following day. Typically, Marietta preferred to stay at a hotel rather than at a friend's home "no matter how luxurious . . . or how kind the owners. . . . I always liked to sit 'under my own vine and fig tree,' to have an independent place of my own, from which I could sally out for short visits to my friends whenever I liked, but knew I had my own place waiting for my return."[5] They stayed at a hotel chosen by Mrs. Flack and from there ventured forth for several days to see New York City's best views and Coney Island. The varied amusements and novelties offered to Marietta astonished her. It was precisely the surge of new images that she needed. In a letter to True Williams she raved over the delights she had enjoyed at Fairview, the Flacks' estate, and the kindnesses they had shown her, although she felt the pull of her rural place: "But I must go home soon anyway—I feel like a new creature since I have been here—the perfect rest—since I have recovered from my tower to N. Y.—is doing me so much good that I think I can write all the better when I do get home."[6]

The first week in August she returned to the family cottage outside of Pierrepont Manor. She stayed long enough to be certain that everything was well cared for and that Finy was fine. Within days she repacked her grip and was off again. In the next fourteen days she passed through Niagara Falls, Montreal, and Saratoga Springs; saw Lake George and Lake Champlain; and came back via the Thousand Islands route.[7] As though her hunger for something outside her narrow district had been sated, she went home. The summer season had ended, but Marietta had seen it pass as a tourist rather than as a farmer. With her characteristic vigor renewed, she went back to work on her projects. She spent the winter of 1881–82 organizing the Holley Library in Adams and rewriting the play *Betsey Bobbet*.

True Williams, who had been acting in Holley's behalf all summer in New York City, had finally made a connection with a Mr. Cox who was eager to see the play. Holley sent him a copy as it had appeared locally with the assurance that she would not want to see it put upon the New York City stage without some changes. Frank Bliss had been approached by the New York Opera Company about the play. They requested a copy of the book *Betsey Bobbet* so that they might write their own script, but Holley recognized that once she gave that company such freedom, her own chances or rights for presenting the play would be surrendered. Meanwhile a woman in the West had offered Holley twenty-five percent of the profits if her husband were given the play to stage at his own expense, in his own manner. Although she was tempted, Holley told Williams, "I would rather not have it on the stage at all than to have it badly played and maybe a failure."[8] Her business sense and her friendships were sometimes confused, in part because she depended for guidance on acquaintances who seemed to know the workings of the New York City and Philadelphia literary worlds. While Bliss and Williams were negotiating over the play in New York, the actor Neil Burgess took a more direct approach: he went to the playwright.

In mid-March Burgess arrived in person in Adams. Of course Holley knew of him since he had created the character Widow Bedott on stage. He had written to Holley announcing that he was about to go on the road with a play titled *Betsey Bobbet*. Holley's lawyer, I. L. Hunt, wrote Burgess a letter asserting that she had the copyright on the name, and he could not do anything about a play without consulting Miss Holley. The two met at Hungerford's in Adams. Convinced that he would do a fair and funny re-creation of Samantha and her friends for the stage, Holley was willing to let him use the names of her famous characters in a play that he would write or arrange to have written. For that privilege he was to pay her a fair sum weekly. She also stipulated that there be nothing "coarse or off color" as she thought there had been in one of his previous plays, *County Fair*. Because she was soon to be off to Claverack for a visit, she had Burgess send the contract there for her signature. It all seemed in order, so she signed it. Had she been at home, with Hungerford or Hunt available to discuss the matter, she might have reconsidered the terms, but in the atmosphere of the Flacks' Fairview she was less shrewd than she should have been.[9]

Having resolved the legal matter, she ended her visit to hurry back to her home. Word had reached her that the humorist Bob Burdette was going to be in nearby Belleville again to entertain the populace with his public lecture, the immensely successful "Rise and Fall of the Mustache." He had been through there on the circuit in February 1881, doing the same speech, and from the podium he had humbly announced that "it was with some hesitation that he had come to lecture so near the home of one whose humor was so much more brilliant than his own . . . Miss Holley." Still unused to having attention called to her in public, Marietta had sat in the audience blushing so that her face "rivalled a full bloom peony."[10] Now a year and a half later Burdette announced that he was bringing with him on the trip his wife, son, and sister-in-law, "Samantha no doubt being the guiding star that draws them . . . and we hope to have the pleasure of meeting her."[11] Holley arrived in time for the lecture and a visit. A mutual regard blossomed. Holley was especially struck by the tenderness that Burdette displayed in the care of his invalid wife, but it was his skill as a raconteur with commonsense humor that won her respect and affection. As they left the tea table, where he had enthralled the party with his special drollery, he began to tremble with stage fright, a response that Holley knew well.[12] Like many of the humorists, including Artemus Ward, Josh Billings, and Twain, Burdette was known by many as a lecturer as much as a writer. They could make a comfortable living by augmenting their writing with lectures. By 1883 Burdette was commanding $150 to $250 a night.[13] During a lecture it was easy for audiences to discern that the humorist was adopting a persona to distinguish between the writer and the character created. But Holley, with her timidity, could not take to the platform, so the confusion between Marietta and Samantha persisted. Even her friends saw the similarities. Soon after the Burdettes' visit, he wrote a sketch of her and sent her a copy.

> Josiah Allen's Wife is a lady with a pleasant, attractive face, quiet and almost childlike in its frank expression. Handsome, yes, very friendly, eloquent eyes that see everything and all the peculiarities of form and expression that come within the range of their quiet speaking glances. The dark brown hair falls in kindly little curls and pretty rings over a broad, white forehead. The smile that lights her face at intervals displays small, regular teeth, and when she speaks, just a

> perceptible lisp, barely perceptible, lends an additional charm to a low, soft voice. Josiah Allen's Wife is Miss Holley![14]

Whatever Holley felt about being identified with Samatha, she was anxious to see Neil Burgess' image of her on the stage. The play opened in June in Providence, Rhode Island, and Holley and Mrs. Flack went down from Claverack for the opening night performance. Burgess played Samantha while his wife took Tirzah Ann's part. Holley was thrilled with Burgess' rendering of Samantha's character as well as with the full house that shook the theater with its applause and handkerchief-waving approval at the conclusion. The work was unquestionably a success as far as Holley was concerned.

She returned to the farm well satisfied that when the play opened in New York City in the autumn, after the Burgesses returned from Europe, her characters and their country patois would continue to charm the sophisticated audiences that Burgress drew. In the meantime she was working on her short fiction, writing and selecting pieces for her first collection of stories. With little of the summer left, she was also overseeing the hasty remodeling of the barn. The previous January her horse had fallen and broken its leg while being driven up Giddings Bridge Hill and had to be shot. The new team of cream horses and the phaeton that replaced the buggy required a larger stable area.[15] Gradually Holley was acquiring some of the accoutrements of her wealth. The new team and rig also made it necessary for her to hire a man to handle them. A local man with that skill and a willingness to do general work was found.

The Holley place was less and less a farm. The garden harvests were more apt to be violets and chrysanthemums than corn and snap beans as her interest in floriculture grew. Besides the few vegetables needed to feed the smaller household, Marietta cultivated food for her spirit by planting flowers in the terrace garden and the angles around the cottage. Lilacs and climbing roses bloomed through the short season, nearly hiding the simple shingled house in an abundance of fragrance and color. The land still had its hold on Marietta. She needed to work on it, but her new association with the genteel lifestyles of her friends gave her an appreciation for the other uses which the soil could be put to. Growing flowers meant that she had broken away from the bitter necessity of working the land. At last she could sow and weed by choice, producing rare beauty rather than common sustenance. Writing rather than farming had become her livelihood; gardening became her pleasure rather than her work.

The impulse to share what she considered her good fortune—in a particularly significant way—kept her at work on the Holley Library. By the summer of 1882 there were over three hundred books available to be drawn out between 7:00 and 8:00 on Tuesday evenings.[16] It was a modest endeavor, perhaps, but for Holley it meant that others like her would not have to endure the grinding life of the North Country without the solace of books. She felt that she could afford such philanthropy, especially because of the payments that she expected to receive from Burgess.

In spite of a severe upper respiratory illness in early December, Marietta continued to edit her stories. She took time out on 26 December for the wedding of her niece Ella Page to D. Sprague Copeland at Angeline's home across the snow-covered meadow. At the end of the next February 1883, she had *Miss Richard's Boy and Other Stories* ready for the American Publishing Company to put into the press. It was a very different book from her previous ones, although the publisher had again retained True Williams as illustrator. The title page bears Marietta Holley's name, although in brackets underneath appears the phrase "Author of the 'Josiah Allen's Wife's' Books." On the frontispiece is an engraving of her likeness and signature. For the first time her readers would see that Holley was not Samantha Allen. The preface is brief and graceful, with none of the fun Samantha has in hers. Holley explains the presence of her portrait in the preface.

> It was suggested to me by one whose interest in the book is only next to my own, that as the belief was quite universal that "Josiah Allen's Wife's" books were written by a member of the stronger sex, it would be advisable to have my portrait appear in this volume.[17]

The rumor that the writer of the Allen stories was really a man had some credence, particularly in the rural areas. After all, with the notable exception of Whitcher, most humorists were men. For some it was as difficult to believe that a woman had written the books as it was that a woman they *knew* had done it. One old gentleman complimented the Samantha work saying he "had a high opinion of the man who wrote that book." When informed that it was indeed written by a woman, he stubbornly declared, "That book was written by a man." Replied Marietta, "I have always supposed it was a compliment."[18] Others were amazed that Holley could write with such insight about the married state. With her characteristic ingenuous look, she would inquire of the speaker if what she had written was really true, letting him confide to

Marietta Holley, 1883. This engraving was the first likeness of Holley to appear in any of her books. It graced the frontispiece of *Miss Richard's Boy and Other Stories* (Hartford, Ct., 1883).

her how accurate in fact it was. In a very revealing comment, Holley admitted that

> many people expressed surprise that the writer being unmarried could have such knowledge of a man's nature, forgetting that every woman has a father, and usually brothers and other male relatives, and as one writer says: "Catch one man and describe him and you describe the species." And the same thing I suppose can be said of woman.[19]

With the portrait and her name in place of her pseudonym, Holley was giving notice to her fans that she was separate even from the creator of the Samantha stories. In *Miss Richard's Boy* they should expect a different artist as well as a different genre. Even the dedication was distinct from the long-winded, high-minded rhetoric of Josiah Allen's Wife:

TO HER MEMORY
whose love
I cannot think has vanished with her presence,
By her daughter
THE AUTHOR.

Marietta was striking out in a new direction, eager to trade on the popularity of her work as Samantha to win recognition for her sentimental stories written in "good English." This collection contains seventeen of those; a few had been published previously in periodicals, but most had been written since her trip outside the county. All of the stories are typical of the sentimental or domestic fiction that had been written by E. D. E. N. Southworth, Marion Harland, Susan Warner, and even Harriet B. Stowe.

In many ways the stories fit the pattern of women's fiction established by the women sentimental writers. The protagonist is usually a girl on the brink of womanhood, just orphaned or abandoned and left to fend for herself as a schoolteacher, seamstress, piano teacher, or mother's helper. Rather than wallowing in her emotions or surrendering to self-pity, the heroine summons all her will and intelligence in handling her new life. One of the difficulties she wrestles with is her—or the author's—underlying consciousness of class distinctions. The men who appear in the stories are generally either drunken fathers or professional men: lawyers, doctors, and clergy. The reward for the heroine making her way through the perils of self-definition is an appropriate marriage to one of the latter. Sometimes the marriage permits the woman to leave a seamy urban scene. For Holley, using a city as backdrop for her stories was a device she could not have used as convincingly before her excursion to Claverack two years before. The rural-urban tensions that characterized the women's fiction of the 1870s had found its way into Holley's work, although the prejudice against the city was always present in the Samantha stories. Like other sentimental writers, Holley used a young girl or boy to intervene, redeem, convert, or reconcile. Characters kept apart by the soap opera devices of missent or lost letters and overheard but misunderstood conversations rejoice at deathbed reunions. Using these conventional materials, Holley recreated the struggle of a young female ego to overcome the loss of nurture in the loss of her guardian, develop a strong sense of self-worth and independence by making her own way in the world, and then be rewarded with the security of marriage and money.[20] It was a fiction Holley believed in, one that suited her pragmatic feminism.

Some of the pieces in *Miss Richard's Boy* are superficially autobiographical. For example, in "Faith Winslow," a young girl on a farm is restless with the endless drudgery. She feels that her poetic soul is threatened by the brutalizing life and wants to escape, chanting "If I were a man . . ." to keep her spirit up. In "Miss Higgin's Man," a young spinster looks under her bed every night for the man she is terrified she will find there. Professing the belief that men are the most abominable creatures on earth, she spends an inordinate amount of time guarding against them. One night she finds her "man," a seven-year-old runaway boy. She decides to let him stay and, of course, comes to love him and through him be more tolerant of all males. The many correspondences between Holley's experience and the stories demonstrate how nearly she lived her fiction. It was a pattern she trusted in, a life script she expected to be fulfilled, even though—at forty-seven years—her own life seemed stalled. Perhaps her habit of hiding her age was a denial of the inescapable reality that her life was not likely to end in the scripted loving marriage. Yet everything she did at this period bespeaks a sense of satisfaction with her life as it was. She was indeed reconciled. If there was strife, it was for poor Samantha and *Betsey Bobbet*.

When the play had been running for some time in New York City, Holley went to see it. To her horror, Burgess had violated her trust and mutilated the images that Holley had lovingly crafted. Samantha appeared on stage in short skirts riding horseback as depicted in one of Josiah's dreams. Holley's first impulse was to dash out of the theater, but she stayed to see the whole play so that she would know the worst. Burgess had added "grotesque and sensational" elements that destroyed the subtle ironies that Holley felt she had created. He had changed the names of characters slightly (Simon Slimpsey was Simon Simple) and had retitled the play *Vim*. The only things that he had kept intact were the dialogue and the profits. Since he had changed the names, he had ceased sending Holley the royalty.[21] Financially, it was a considerable loss. The play ran for two hundred performances at the Bijou Theater in 1883 and was still being revived in New York City and Boston in 1888.[22] Holley wanted to take legal action against Burgess, but her attorney assured her that it would be a wasteful drain on her time and money, and so she dropped the matter. At least she had the consolation that Burgess would suffer from his conscience, a belief she had acquired from both her Bible and her Emerson. Beyond such redress she could hope that the names of her characters and herself had been largely disassociated from the travesty, and her reputation as a sensible rather than sensational writer restored. Meanwhile her modest original version of the drama was still being played in small cities and villages. It had run in Iowa for the benefit of an Episcopal church. Another troupe was performing it in Ohio. At Claverack it played again in the spring of 1882 with the profits going to the Methodist church, clearing in one evening's performance nearly one hundred dollars.[23] Clearly the appeal of Holley's rustic philosophers was strong enough to survive any injury that Burgess' burlesque might have done to it.

In early April 1883 Holley made her first extended trip to New York City, primarily to visit her friends the Newmans. Again preferring private apartments to quarters shared with friends, she took accommodations at the Oriental, a hotel run by two maiden ladies, the Misses Underhill. It was across the street from the Astor Library, on Astor Place, and had a slight reputation for being a literary center because several of the women who stayed there were writers—or "scribblers." Amid elegance of the sort that Marietta called "solid old style magnificence," she occupied the most spacious and grand front rooms for a while, then removed to a back room, number 14, that had a window opening onto a courtyard, beyond which was a Broadway theater. Having chosen the room because it was so far removed from the street noises and housekeeping bustle, she was pleased with the daytime quiet that allowed her to write uninterrupted. At night, however, after she retired to bed, she would hear distant singing from the theater, but it was no annoyance, only a charming curiosity.

It was during one of the periods when severe colds and respiratory ailments kept Holley from her work that she was wakened suddenly in the early morning by a bright glow at the window. The theater was afire, and the winds were scattering cinders to the roofs of the Oriental. She snatched from under her pillow the handkerchief in which she always tied up her purse and jewelry. Flinging her long cloak over her nightdress, she stuffed the parcel into her coat pocket, then began to consider what to take next. By then firemen and male guests were arriving in the hallway to help. To one man she entrusted the manuscript of a book that she had nearly finished. Assured that she would have time to escape, she threw her best clothes and her books into a trunk, covered her curl papers with her bonnet, and hurried out.[24]

The fire was contained, and Holley was finally reestablished in her room. When she began to recover from that shock, the business of her literary life accelerated again. Bliss and the directors of the American Publishing Company had offered Holley a trip to Europe, certainly as a gift, but very likely in the hope that she would write about Samantha in Europe. Holley was in New York City, surrounded by friends to whom a trip to Europe was of little more consequence than the trip from Pierrepont Manor to New York was for Holley. She was very near to accepting the offer, in spite of her dread of deep water, which she attributed in part to her Uncle Christopher Taber's death at sea. She recognized that her fear was unreasonable to most people, but she couldn't seem to overcome it. As she had Samantha tell Josiah, "Mebby I shall be drowned on dry land, but I don't believe it." At the urging of her friends, she bought a steamer trunk and arranged for the companionship of a young woman who had been educated abroad. At the end of May, before the tickets were purchased, she returned home briefly. The apprehensions and foreboding of her family rekindled the fear that she had been stifling. That, as much as their disapproval, killed her resolve to go. The trip was canceled and the steamer trunk became a clothespress.[25]

After a month or so at the farm, Holley set off for a visit to Claverack. It was July, and there was an outbreak of diphtheria in the Adams area. Whole families came down with the illness. By 18 July five persons were dead. Soon after Marietta arrived at the Flacks', she was stricken with a chill that lasted four or five hours, after which appeared other symptoms that might have indicated diphtheria. Although Marietta begged to be sent to a hospital so she would not infect the household, Mrs. Flack insisted on setting her up in a room where she herself could oversee Marietta's care. The patient was despondent, which only exacerbated her symptoms and fears. Dr. Flack would appear at her chamber door cheerfully insisting that it was *not* "malignant diphtheria" that she had, but she noted that every article removed from her room was disinfected and she overheard two of the domestics discussing her illness, one intoning, "She has got death in her face."[26] It was a terribly dark time, especially for a woman inclined to an inordinate concern with her health. Gradually the illness itself began to abate, and the studied good humor of the Flack family eased Holley out of her depression. By mid-August she was sufficiently well to take short trips out with Mrs. Flack, venturing as far as Albany, then even to the Newmans' summer home at Round Lake, where she spent a week. The Adirondak air restored her entirely so that she felt well enough to return home to the farm and resume her work there while she continued recuperating. While resting at home, in her hammock, she somehow fell, seriously injuring her head, neck, and shoulders.[27] For a time she retired to the quiet of the farm cottage to allow her body to heal before she resumed work on the manuscript that she had saved from the Oriental fire.

The autumn of 1883 was quiet for the Holley sisters. They had a young man to help with the horses and do other general chores. Marietta had moved downstairs into the room off the parlor that her mother had occupied, so the hired man was given the upstairs room over the parlor, which was partially filled with papers and stored goods. The man had been known to be careless about fire—a dangerous trait in a farmhand—and had nearly set the house ablaze twice. Marietta had taken to giving him a light by which he could get up to bed, then having him set it outside his door so that she could take it away. On the night of 26 November she did that as usual. In the middle of the night she was wakened by a commanding sense that she must go into the parlor and look up through the stovepipe hole in the ceiling. There was a fire in the room above. Rousing Finy, Marietta rushed to get the man awake and found that a candle that he had secreted in his room had caught the cotton bedspread on fire. The alarm was sounded; neighbors ran to help; and the blaze was extinguished, but not before $125 worth of damage was done to the Holleys' house, furniture, and apparel.[28] Holley was insured for the loss, and the company settled immediately, but the consequences of the fire were immense. The fastness of the farm home seemed lost. There was a renewed sense of vulnerability as there had been when the thief had robbed their barn. More important, Marietta's belief in the presence of departed spirits as agents in her life was reinforced. She felt more strongly than ever that their guidance and protection was available to her. In fact, she believed that it was her departed mother who woke her and commanded her to look for the fire, thereby saving their lives.

More and more Holley sought connection with the spirits, using the Ouija, automatic writing, and even a medium on occasion. All these had been favorite pastimes with the Carletons and many of Holley's women friends in New York City. Although Holley, like Samantha, did not believe in professional mediums who produced seances with theatrical effects, she would sometimes go incognito to speak with a spiritualist medium recommended by her literary friends.[29] Perhaps the parapsychological experiments satisfied a need for mystification. It may have been her reaction to increasing scientific naturalism in art and philosophy. Holley adapted many mechanical and pseudoscientific images to explain her acceptance of spiritualist activities, a technique that many practitioners used to convert a dubious public. The argument might be that if a telegraph could carry a message, so could other unseen impulses. Spiritualism was to be regarded not as *super*natural but *ultra*natural, science and mechanics taken one step further.[30] Her interest in spiritualist activities was compatible with her belief in divine guidance. She was naively prepared to accept both as manifestations of God's way. The same confidence that led her to ask the Ouija questions led her to continue her daily practice of looking into her Bible for advice. Each morning she would open it at random and, without looking, run her thumb down the page. Whatever verse it rested on was the guiding principle or directive for her day. It was a practice that would eventually prove crucial to the aging writer.

That winter repairs were made to the cottage, but no structural changes were undertaken. In January, Will Shaver, the young man who had been Holley's book agent for *My Wayward Pardner,* was married to a young woman from Adams. From February to April Shaver's "magic view entertainment and great moral show" played to small gatherings around the southern part of the county. It appears that he had given up canvassing to become an itinerant showman of some sort. Whatever friendship Holley and Shaver had was strained by his choice of work and his inclination to drink.

Marietta, nearing forty-nine, was going about her usual winter schedule of writing in the mornings. Thursday evenings she attended Baptist prayer meetings in Adams. If there was a lecture she was interested in, she would go in her own conveyance. Josh Billings' speech in Belleville in January 1884 was one she was not likely to miss. In rare clear weather she might go to Mannsville, five miles south along the state road, to visit the Ford family, but for the most part Adams was the center of her social life when she was in the North Country.

General Hungerford and Holley continued to work on the expansion of the library together and support the intellectual growth in the village. His genial, openhanded character and her intensity and timidity made theirs an interesting partnership. By the spring of 1884 they had accomplished a good deal. Then one May day, having business in Watertown, Hungerford set out to take the 12:52 train. He had eaten his usual hearty noon meal and was running late. As he sprinted to catch the train, he tripped, fell, but regained his feet and boarded. The sixty-six-year-old man never quite recovered himself, and the train personnel took him off at Adams Center, three miles up the line. His wife was summoned. Within two hours he suffered an attack of some kind and died. Before Marietta even knew he was ill, he was gone.[31]

As though to compensate for her personal loss, Holley's professional responsibilities increased. She was at work on the manuscript that would bring together the themes of suffrage and temperance: *Sweet Cicely*. A letter from Susan B. Anthony two weeks after Hungerford's death congratulated Holley on the work in progress. Anthony and Stanton were working on the third volume of *The History of Woman Suffrage* and wanted to be sure Holley's fictional "hapless woman" suffered under all the legal disabilities that Anthony listed—defined by relationship to men as daughter, as wife (with a scathing reference to Tilton), as mother, and as citizen. Anthony encouraged her to use all the incidents of outrage available, including the false teeth story that Anthony told at her trial, which "brought the house down." As the story goes, a wife got new dentures, but they were improperly made, so they caused her great pain and distorted her looks. The husband sued, but the wife could not testify. On their day in court, her husband was feeling mean, so he said that the teeth fit her just fine, and she was stuck with them. Marietta retold it in *Sweet Cicely* in a catalogue of terrible—but legal—injustices done to women by their husbands.[32]

While the feminist front was seeking her support, the publishers of periodicals were courtng her. In September 1884 Cyrus H. K. Curtis sent Holley a copy of the *Ladies' Home Journal* followed by a letter expressing the hope that she liked the magazine and would be interested in furnishing "matter" for its columns. He boasted that they expected to print 200,000 copies of the December issue, adding, "Our aim is to make it the *best* and most *helpful* practical home Journal yet published. Will you help us?"[33] One month later, S. S. McClure was announcing his intention to secure the most popular American writers to supply fiction for the syndicate he was forming. His urgent, audacious letter of 20 October proposes these terms: to pay at least what the best magazines were paying and, if receipts exceeded that sum, to pay all but ten percent of the excess to the writer. He insisted his motive was in part to secure the field for American writers who had been neglected for the English novelists. He offered Holley the copyright so that she could publish the stories later as she wished. Five days later another letter followed saying he needed between three hundred and four hundred stories a year. Offering to change the terms and pay only a fixed price in cash, he urged her to respond and negotiate. A later post the same day brought this simple note: "Dear Miss Holley, Please write to me definitely as soon as possible."[34]

McClure was an imaginative, enterprising publisher who was willing to take bold risks. He was forming a syndicate out of which would eventually emerge *McClure's Magazine*. His strategies were to buy manuscripts from celebrated authors and sell his magazines cheaper than his competitors—ten cents and twelve-and-a-half cents rather than twenty-five cents and thirty-five cents. His hurry was contrary to the languid manner of the rural Yankee who did business slowly, carefully, and often socially. What answer Holley sent McClure is lost, but a letter dated 15 December from him has an almost apologetic air, in spite of its intent.

> I am very sorry to hear you are sick. If I can serve you in any way, please call on me. I do not wish to intrude business matters on you and write this only that you may attend to it when you can. I should like to print a chapter from your book and if you are too unwell to copy it I would be glad to select and copy it myself.[35]

Immediately after New Year's Day, Holley went into New York City to visit her friends, returning to rooms at the Oriental. There McClure visited her, and whatever reservations she may have felt because of his correspondence were somewhat allayed when he offered to buy the serial rights to "The Pound Party" for $100. He requested changes in the manuscript, which she made; but before she delivered it to McClure, Marion Harland called on her and warned her that McClure had never paid her for a story of hers he had used, and she advised Holley to get the money in advance. Holley enlisted the aid of her friend the publisher Hubbard to deliver the story and collect the cash. When Hubbard told McClure that he was not to leave the manuscript without receiving the money, McClure returned "The Pound Party." The agreement she had signed on 13 May 1885 was worthless.[36]

The magazine market had slowly become glutted with short fiction. By 1886 most magazines had many more manuscripts than they could publish in two years. Because it was difficult for a writer to get into the market, the demand for Holley's work is testimony to the value that publishers placed on her popularity. The $100 must have sounded too good to be true to Holley. In the late 1880s even well-known writers were being paid only five dollars a page or about three-fourths of a cent per word by *Leslie's Popular Monthly*, while the weeklies paid five dollars per column.[37]

Holley stayed most of the winter of 1885 in New York City working on the final copy of *Sweet Cicely*. In March she left for Claverack to attend the funeral of her friend Alonzo Flack, who had died suddenly of pneumonia.[38] The funeral oration was quickly becoming a familiar litany for Marietta. It was almost inevitable that as the youngest child in the family she would witness the deaths of her elders, but to lose her contemporaries so suddenly was a shock too often repeated in these middle years.

The friendship with Will Carleton and his wife was still vital. As though he knew she needed his light touch just then, he wrote her from Brooklyn about their settling into their house, ending with a vigorous dash: "Work—work—work! When shall we reach that portion of Heaven set off as playground? And then won't we have a small eternity of sports and pastimes (or passeternities, I suppose it will be then)."[39]

Holley returned to the farm in the spring in time for her cousin Henry's visit. He stayed with his father, Marietta's aged Uncle David, and visited with all the relatives. He and his literary cousin had much to discuss. The second edition of his book *The Politicans* was being published, and he had a new work ready to go to press titled *Heggensville Papers*. Henry spent the entire summer in the vicinity, and it appears that Marietta did likewise. In early autumn *Sweet Cicely* was ready for publication by Funk and Wagnalls, although there were delays because the book was being published simultaneously in London and New York City to secure the English and Canadian copyrights. Funk and Wagnalls published in trade, not by subscription, but seven thousand copies had been sold before the date of issue. Although Holley was recovering from a severe attack of fever described as "malarial," she rejoiced in the reception of her latest book.[40] Susan B. Anthony wrote a loving letter thanking the author for *Sweet Cicely*.

> We have read it aloud here [in Washington]—Miss Spofford and I and her sisters and laughed until we cried over it!! A very bright newspaper scribbler in Philadelphia—Miss Anna McDowell—says she cannot stand it much longer with *Josiah*—it is time to kill him off and for Samantha to marry a *smarter* man!![41]

Anthony again urged Holley to come to Washington, D.C., and give a "real earnest talk to Congress in person!! I believe you could speak if you would try." Her letter ends with a tender recollection of their meeting in Adams years before. Holley had also sent Rose Cleveland, the president's sister, a copy of *Sweet Cicely: Josiah Allen as a Politician*. Funk and Wagnalls had published Rose's book *The Long Run* the previous year after Holley had directed her to them. In the letter that accompanied the book, Holley first praised Cleveland's essay, then wrote that she knew Cleveland was interested in temperance and wanted to know if she liked the book. Holley was also interested in knowing how Rose Cleveland, from her position inside the White House, felt about the political shenanigans described. In return, Rose Cleveland sent a perfunctory note saying that she had read the book in stolen time and had thoroughly enjoyed it.[42]

The Cicely of the title is Josiah's niece. The sketch of her that adorns the frontispiece where Holley's portrait had appeared in the previous book looks somewhat like Marietta herself. Cicely is the victim of drink because she married a man named Slide who died a drunkard. From the outset, Cicely's plight is described in chapters that alternate with chapters on Washington politics. Cicely's difficulty is that the property and money of her deceased husband are being used by his executor for saloons while she has no control over it. Her powerlessness is further defined by the dangers she foresees for her son if Demon Drink is allowed to continue to flow in the Union. The temperance novel had become a genre unto itself by 1885, often written by men and usually "intertwined with woman's fiction when it center[ed] on the feminine victims."[43] At the convention of the American Temperance Union in Saratoga Springs in August 1836, 400 delegates from nineteen states and territories had formally endorsed fiction as a weapon in the crusade against alcohol.[44] Holley and the other temperance writers accepted that directive as readily as Holley adopted Frances Willard's argument that running the government was really just "enlarged housekeeping." Suffrage was becoming not just the reform sought, but a means to all the reforms women could accomplish with the vote.[45] In *Sweet Cicely* Samantha wrestles with the plight of the woman temperance worker who is still without political power. At the same time Samantha suffers her own difficulties with Josiah, who has decided that he wants to run for senator because he has the principles of a politician. Samantha reflects: "I thought of the powerful blasts of temptation that blowed through them broad streets, and the small size of my pardner, and the light weight of his bones and principles."[46] After settling a dispute about whether the figure of Liberty on the new Jonesville courthouse should be male or female, and preparing the inside of her head instead of the outside by reading, studying, and re-reading *Foxe's Book of Martyrs*. Samantha sets out to examine Washington, D.C. As soon as possible, she visits the president, Chester Arthur, then passes along from politician to politician sounding them out on their platforms. She describes with her usual earthy metaphors the sights and sounds of the city and vicinity.

Many of the elements of the sentimental novel are mingled with Holley's temperance message as well as her implicit criticism of Washington politics. What is newest in this work is the focus on spiritualism. Cicely, who is bound by literary convention to die, has a psychic vision of her aunt at the moment of the relative's death, and Samantha, who had been a staunch skeptic, begins to believe. There is a long, teary deathbed scene for Cicely, and the book ends with the boy for whom she had such fear of ruination by drink dying of scarlet fever instead. The book was dedicated to sad-eyed mothers like Cicely, but its appeal was wider than that. In eight weeks 12,000 copies had been sold; over the following two years it went through eight editions. Frances Willard compared the work to some of Dickens': "All the humor—the quaintness, the keen insight, the originality of her other books is found here while in addition there is a depth of Pathos—a power of striking hard blows with a velvet gloved hand—not shown in any of her previous works."[47] Will Carleton called it her greatest success.[48] It is one of her strongest works, showing Holley at the peak of her ability to handle the rustic humor, the temperance genre, and the sentimental-domestic novel all at once in an almost seamless narrative.

Holley had earned a rest. While she spent the winter at home, Rose Cleveland continued to write her from Holland Patent, near Rome, New York, and her winter home in Florida encouraging Holley to consider a home in another climate. However, Marietta was improving the cottage instead. Adams provided enough diversions. Beecher was lecturing nearby again in May, an event that she would not miss. By then, the railroad had sleeping cars making the run into New York City daily, so it became easier for Holley to make brief trips in to see the Newmans when they were available. On one visit during the spring, she met the portrait artist Theodore Pine, who many years before had painted the portrait of the man for whom Pierrepont Manor was named. Pine was a deacon in Bishop Newman's church. At Newman's urging, Holley sat for Pine in the mornings until, in June, the life-sized portrait was finished.[49] It was briefly on display at the Academy of Design, where Holley's friend Hillary Bell complained that the expression was all wrong: "Too tame, too self-satisfied.—You might have known how it would be. The idea of having a Deacon paint a portrait. . . . You should at least have sent him off on a spree before he commenced it."[50] In the portrait she wears a delicate white lace gown that flows around her figure. The lavishly ruffled bodice is ornamented simply by pink roses, Holley's favorite flower. Diamonds add glitter on her left hand and to her ears, but the mood of the painting is calm and reconciled. Her hands rest on a book, perhaps a Bible. Her hair, which is still only flecked with gray, curls around her high forehead. As usual it is her eyes that catch and hold one's attention. Whatever may have been amiss with the rest of the portrait, the eyes are right. The straightforward gaze is tinged with humor, but the eyes have a look that still bespeaks a sorrow never shared.

When her business in New York City was concluded, Holley visited her friends at Claverack in June. In July she rejoined the Newmans at their summer home at Round Lake, briefly breaking away to join in the memorial service for the Reverend Mr. Flack and the unveiling of his monument. At the end of the month, she went to Sartoga Springs.[51]

The racing season was on, but Holley was able to find comfortable accommodations, first with Miss Augusta Wiggins. She was a deaconess in the Episcopal Church, a devout woman who kept an altar for private devotions in her home, took Holley to early morning service, and stood to say grace. For Holley, the experience of that week with Wiggins was enlightening and enjoyable. Nevertheless Holley preferred her own place, so she found a quiet room at the top of a boardinghouse, where she passed the remainder of the golden summer. Her earlier short visits to Saratoga had given her the ideas she needed to commence the book that she subtitled *Flirtin' with Fashion,* and she immersed herself in the ambiance of the racing resort. She wrote every morning high above the noises of street and servants. She preferred to be left alone, so her morning's ration of the vitalizing springwater was left outside her door. The muse was kind; the book was written quickly. At the end of a day's drafting she went below to take her meals, often meeting the Newmans or other of her acquaintances. She listened to the chatter of chambermaids and hall boys, col-

The Pine Portrait. Holley commissioned this portrait by Theodore Pine in 1885. It now hangs in the Flower Memorial Library, Watertown, New York.

lecting the images that furnished the background for the adventures of *Samantha at Saratoga*. Like the country girl she was at heart, she found a hiking companion, Sophie Smith, and the two women set out to walk all over Saratoga "with the zeal and determination of early discoverers."[52] Quiet side streets, the halls of the springs, even an ancestral haunted house were visited by the Tramps, as the friends were called. Then there were garden parties, socials in the lighted fairyland of the park, music, and delicate foods. With her writing going so well, and she herself having a splendid time, Holley felt vigorous, productive, and satisfied.

She had promised the work to Hubbard of Philadelphia, although other publishers were eager to get it. J. S. Ogilvie of New York City sent Holley a box of flowers then arrived himself to try to win the advantage, but she remained firm in her commitment to Hubbard. The next February a book appeared on the market bearing her pseudonym: Ogilvie had put out a volume titled *Miss Jones's Quilting and Other Stories*. One had to read the title page very closely to discover that only the title story was by Josiah Allen's Wife. The piece was pirated from *My Opinions and Betsey Bobbet's* in which it had appeared as the chapter "The Minister's Bedquilt." The remainder of the book is trash. Holley's publisher encouraged her to sue Ogilvie, but such an action would have required her to appear in court. Holley, with some shame at her failure of principle over shyness, felt that she could endure the injustice better than the trial.

The deal with Hubbard had been struck because his price, $10,000 in cash, had seemed the best. Cyrus Curtis, editor of the *Ladies' Home Journal*, bought serial rights to several chapters, an arrangement that Hubbard at first agreed to. Illustrations were made, several chapters published, and one more was ready to go to press when Hubbard rushed to Saratoga Springs to consult with the author. He had reconsidered, fearing that the serial publication would severely diminish sales of the book. He had already advanced Holley half the sum for the book, with the rest to be paid when the final manuscript was delivered. He insisted that unless she stopped the next chapter from appearing, he would pay her no more. Holley immediately left for Philadelphia to discuss the matter with Curtis, who she felt was a reliable friend as well as publisher. The illustrations for the next segment of *Samantha at Saratoga* were already engraved. He had paid that expense and the price of the manuscript. Holley's solution was to write a new story to fit Curtis' illustrations, a feat that she accomplished in three days. He returned the chapter Hubbard required, and the issue was settled. Holley returned to Saratoga with the final $5,000 in hand.[53]

Back in Saratoga she rested, seeking the entertainment that she feared and yet sought: the play with psychic matters. Behind her hotel a palmist had set up a tent in the midst of a garden. A sign on the tent bore a quotation from the Bible: "In her left hand is wisdom and in her right length of days." In *Samantha at Saratoga,* Josiah Allen's Wife had visited a palmist at an Indian encampment, a woman who did her work in a tent with verses of Scripture painted on it, and that woman had told Samantha wonderful things as well as some that were patently false. Marietta, like Samantha, didn't trust professional spiritualists or occultists, but the biblical reference overcame her reticence. Mrs. Newman went along, and after having her reading done first, she was enthusiastic about what she had been told. Marietta was surprised to find a woman "with a pale spiritual face, not looking at all like the ordinary fakir fortune teller." Holley recorded that the woman seemed perplexed: "I can't make it out. You are not a teacher or a preacher but yet your words seem to go all around the world." That may not have convinced Marietta, because it could so easily have been that the woman recognized the author, but what followed startled her. "You are thinking of leaving the house you are living in now. You had better, for it is not healthy."[54] The fortune-teller had hit her mark precisely. In spite of the improvements Marietta had made, the farmhouse was an aging wooden structure that was damp because it was set right on the ground. Holley's health seemed threatened. She had begun to consider building a new home but had not yet formulated the plan. After all, the seventy-three-year-old cottage was her father's house, built with his own hands. Nevertheless, it was dangerously prone to fire and it held the dampness. In the high, airy hotel room, Holley considered the woman's words.

After sharing Thanksgiving with the Newmans, she went on to New York City to spend the winter. She had given up staying at the Oriental, and eventually the Murray Hill Hotel became her unofficial New York City residence. The Carletons were living in Brooklyn, the Newmans at a nearby hotel. Holley continued to sit on the fringe of a group made up primarily of publishers, women writers such as Ella Wheeler Wilcox and Frances Hodgson Burnett, and noted clergy. The Newmans and Carletons remained closest, however. Will had endeared himself to her with his sincere devotion to his mother. After some bit of tomfoolery with Marietta and his wife, Will would chuckle, "Now I will go down to let mother scold me. It will do her so much good."[55] They all joined Holley at the Murray Hill for breakfasts and exchanged evening visits. Carleton understood Holley's feelings when Henry Ward Beecher died that March while she was in New York. He arranged to take her out to the cemetery to visit the flower-covered grave so she might pay her last respects to Beecher as she wished.

That done, Holley began the trip to Washington, D.C., that she had been planning since the previous autumn. After settling in at the Willard Hotel, she set about meeting all the women of influence, wives of generals and presidents, whom Mrs. Newman knew in Washington. An invitation to the White House to meet Mrs. Cleveland was forthcoming. On 31 March Marietta Holley arrived at the White House, the very same one which Samantha Smith Allen had boldly laid siege to. Mrs. Cleveland chatted with the writer for nearly half an hour, inviting her back for the following Saturday to meet the president at a reception in the East Room.[56] As usual, Holley kept apart from the throng of visitors, watching the crowd, recording her impressions and verifying for herself the notions she had brought with her. Like Samantha, she was impressed with the variety of Americans, awed by the fact that democracy could bring them together.

Having greeted Cleveland, Holley was about to leave when his wife invited Marietta to step into the conservatory and pick for herself whatever flowers she wanted from the abundance of native and exotic blossoms there. It was a gesture that touched Holley deeply, and she took away with her more than just the small bouquet. There was finally affirmation of her worth as an American, a woman, and a writer.[57]

On the first excursion to Washington, D.C., Holley met many of the notables of the Capital's political and social sets, but the friends were more nearly acquaintances. One lasting relationship began when she met Clara Barton at the Riggs House through a mutual friend.[58] Clara and Marietta seemed destined to be intimates. Besides their political views and feminist concerns, the two women shared fundamental life experiences and habits in spite of their physical differences. Clara was the youngest child in her family just as Marietta was, separated from her siblings by ten years, and both women had been painfully shy as children. Barton was fifteen years older and more robust from birth, having "acquired strength out of all proportion to her five feet and feminine roundness." Whereas Marietta was weak but agile, Clara was strong, able to "lift to her shoulders a full keg of cider." Like Holley, she knew she was not beautiful but that men found her attractive. However, early in her life she had decided not to marry.[59]

As a child of six Clara had begun to write verses, and although she recognized how little merit they had, she continued to write them throughout her life even when her journal keeping and prolific correspondence threatened to choke the poet's impulse. By the time she was forty-five she knew that she would enjoy a writer's life but that it was too late to begin seriously. Her wish to write was insufficient: except for some necessity or an "intense inspiration," she would postpone writing to do almost anything else.[60] Unlike Holley, she lacked the drive, and she had another avenue open to her: the lecture circuit. In the late 1860s Barton had joined forces with Susan B. Anthony and had befriended Frances Willard. Her efforts in procuring and distributing supplies on battlefronts, her work among the soldiers during the Civil War, and her concern for alleviating suffering wherever war or disaster struck fused with her consciousness that woman suffrage was a necessity for a better world. Unwilling to discipline herself to write for her causes, she chose lecturing. She loathed the actual time spent on the platform: "All speech-making terrifies me. First, I have no taste for it, and lastly I hate it."[61] What she loved was native American humor, particularly Josh Billings, Twain, and "Samanthy." At home with her family and friends in Dannsville, New York, she would read Twain aloud to them to cheer them up. After the shooting of President Garfield, she retired from the heat and worry to read Samantha's words for comfort.[62] By the time the author of those words and Barton finally met, they had long admired each other. Thus began a loving friendship, conducted mostly through their correspondence, that lasted until Clara's death. After this first meeting, they did not see each other again for seven years because of Barton's hectic work on behalf of the Red Cross. Meanwhile Holley's own travels took her to new vistas.

Elinor Scott was on the "tower" with Holley when the two women accepted an invitation from a friend of Mrs. U. S. Grant to visit Virginia. Going by way of Baltimore, Holley and her companion arrived at Point Comfort, the Saratoga of the South, near Fortress Monroe. The women checked in at the Hygeia Hotel, but the only room immediately available was a large one that they would have to share. Holley refused, preferring to wait all day until a single room was ready. It was late in the evening when she was finally escorted to a small room on a distant, gloomy corridor by a black man, "the largest and blackest I had ever seen."[63] She was somewhat comforted to discover the next morning that the writer Marion Harland was just a few doors away, and the daylight swept away some of the misgivings that Holley felt. She had never been so near a military base before, and she took advantage of the opportunity to study the very real soldiers who had previously lived in her imagination as the patriots and armed farmers of her father's stories. Her Civil War memories were stirred by a visit to the national cemetery and an old soldiers home nearby.

Curiosity was gnawing at Holley, so she hired a rig and a "colored driver" to go out into the countryside. Northerners were becoming aware that Negro suffrage in the South had inherent difficulties that southern whites were not resolving quickly or easily. Magazines were starting to print fiction and essays depicting the plight of freed blacks, which included atrocities physical, moral, and legal. Holley had accepted abolitionist Wendell Phillips' promise "First the Negro, then the woman,"[64] and she grew anxious about the progress of the former because she was impatient with the lack of progress for the latter. Her solitary excursion into the Virginia countryside provided her with a chance to see the consequences of suffrage. She stopped to visit at the "colored school" at Hampton. She passed the decaying plantations with separate slave quarters. She had never known Negroes; there were almost no black people in Jefferson County. In spite of her abolitionist views, they had been an abstraction to her. In Adams when she had met Frederick Douglas at Hungerford's, her reaction had been ambivalent. Although she admired his intellect and perseverance, she felt that "it did seem strange to find such great qualities hidden in such a dark envelope."[65] To Holley, the little homesteads of the blacks, with their cabins and tidy gardens, stood in bold contrast to the dilapidated plantation mansions as proof that "Freedom and Liberty were beginning their work."[66] It was her first close contact with the facts of life for southern blacks. She carefully recorded the images of freed women ploughing their own fields with "wooly-headed little urchins" in tow.[67] Holley returned to Washington, D.C., and then home via New York City with a fresh perspective on the race question.

In July she retired from the heat of the cities to the coolness of her tree-shaded house. Within days she was severely ill. At first she had only a cold, but it quickly became acute bronchitis, and pneumonia seemed imminent. Her doctor advised her to go to Sartoga Springs, but it was several weeks before she was well enough to be up to chat with friends, and it was not until the end of August that she could be out driving. Her latest book, *Samantha at Saratoga or Flirtin' with Fashion,* dedicated to the Summer Tramps, was finally out after a delay to obtain English copyright.[68] When she was well enough to travel, Marietta took the train to the resort city she loved and the friends who loved her. She had been so ill that she had not even written to her friends in New York City. Will Carleton had penned a note in July saying he hoped the poems she was working on would be out in time for the holidays, adding, "They will broaden your reputation, and show to the public that other side of you—weird and pathetic."[69] When he finally learned of her illness, Carleton wrote her a cheering letter telling her how he had been "laughing and grieving" over the Saratoga book, calling one of her character's names "a corker—a triumph of nomenclature." The letter is tinged with envy, though, when he tells her that the book is worth even more than she got paid for it, and that "there are authors enough who would swell with pride if they could get half that sum for a book."[70]

Publishers were still demanding her sketches and stories. The Bacheller Syndicate was offering $50 for a 1,200-word piece; The *Yankee Blade* was willing to pay $500 for a story that would cover no more than four pages because "a short story from you is as valuable as a long one."[71] Nevertheless, Funk and Wagnalls had agreed to publish a volume of her poems. At last she hoped to find recognition for the work that she considered to be the most worthy. The volume appeared in time for the holidays, December 1887. The clothbound edition bears a colorful holly motif on the cover—an obvious pun—but there also appears a black housefly. The title page names Josiah Allen's Wife as the poet, with Marietta's name added parenthetically below. The preface concludes, "The many faults of my verses I can see only too well; their merits, if they have any, I leave with the public—which has always been so kind to me—to discover."[72] Like the other one of her books that deviated from Samantha's accustomed style, this one is dedicated to Holley's mother. Most of the poems were written when she was publishing in the *Jefferson County Journal,* although some appear revised or with new titles. Nothing about them is truly new, however, and the book was mainly a curiosity to her reading public.

Holley sent a copy to Rose Cleveland, who responded with faint praise.[73] The poet had more success with John Greenleaf Whittier, to whom she also sent a volume of the poems. Whittier was usually very generous in his responses to women writers, even "lavish in his praise."[74] To Holley he wrote in part, "With the wit and wisdom of Josiah Allen's Wife I have long been familiar. I have read thy beautiful poem, 'The Deacon's Daughter,' with moist eyes. It is perfect."[75]

The Deacon's Daughter

The spare room windows wide were raised,
    And could you look that summer's day
On pastures green and sunny hills
    And low rills running away;
Nearer, the square front yard was sweet
    With rose and caraway.

Upon a couch drawn near the light
The deacon's only daughter lay,
Bending upon the distant hills
Her eyes of dark and thoughtful gray.
The blue veins on her forehead show
'Twas wasted so away.

She moved and from her slender hand,
Fell off her mother's wedding ring.
She smiled into her father's face,
"So drops from me each earthly thing,
My hands are free to hold the flowers
Of the eternal spring."

She had ever walked in quiet ways,
Not over beds of flowery ease,
But Sundays in the village choir
She sweetly sang of "Ways of peace,"
Of "Ways of peace and pleasantness,"
She trod such paths as these.

No sweeter voice in all the choir
Praised God in innocence and truth.
The Deacon in his straight-backed pew
Had dreams of her he lost in youth
And thought of fair-faced Hebrew maids,
Of Rachael and of Ruth.

But she had faded day by day,
Growing more mild, and pure, and sweet,
As nearer to her ear there came
A distant sea's mysterious beat
Till now this summer afternoon
Its waters touched her feet.

Upon the painted porch without
Two women whispered low
They thought she'd go out with the day
They said "The Deacon's wife went so."
And then they gently pitied him,
"It was a dreadful blow."

"But she was good, she was prepared,
She would be better off than here."
And then they thought 'twas strange that he,
Her father had not shed a tear.

And then they talked of news
And all the promise of the year.

Her father sat beside the bed
Holding her cold hands tenderly,
And to the everlasting hills
He mutely turned his eyes away,
"My God, my shelter
Oh shadow me today."

He knew not when she crossed the stream
And passed into the land unseen,
So gently did she go from him
Into its pasture still and green,
Into the land of pure delight
And Jordan rolled between.

Then knelt he down beside his dead
His white locks lit with sunset's flame,
"My God! oh leave me not alone,
But blessed be thy holy name."
The golden gates were lifted up.
The King of Glory came.[76]

Holley gratefully acknowledged the compliment, admitting that she had sent "the little volume out with fear and trembling. It seemed almost like putting out a tender little child that I had long carried in my heart—out in the world to receive good or bad usage."[77] Her works were her children, a fact that Marietta, at fifty-two, had accepted.

She hardly had time to enjoy the small acclaim her poems received when she was again in mourning. Her Uncle David, at eighty-five, suffered a brief illness. The aged tale teller failed quickly; within two weeks, he died. On a Sunday morning, 4 March, he fell asleep and never awoke. Marietta had faced loss often, even one closer, but the insistence of death as a presence in her life was hard on her.

That spring Holley made her decision concerning the house. She hired W. H. Wheeler of Adams to build her a $3,500 house and engaged David Gaylord as the architect. For a year or more Holley's friends had been speculating that she would buy a home in New York City or Washington, D.C., but the truth was that she would not or could not leave the homestead. It suited her need for solitary spaces and friendly distances. The new dwelling, which she insisted on calling a cottage, was to be built just a few rods north of the farmhouse, the same distance from the gravel highway on the other side of the rail fence. Her time was thoroughly occupied with the design of the house. From Will Carleton she received a loving reproach.

> There is a theory in this house that you owe almost every body in it a letter. . . .
>
> This is not written to find out if you are well, young lady, for we heard that you were, and that you were building a huge cottage upon your paternal estate, with rooms in it for all your friends. . . . They showed us too a beautiful book, with holly-wreaths on the cover, and Holley flowers within, and of course we became furiously angry because you didn't send us one. So you see, taking it all together, what a high old scrape you're in. And I can't contrive any other way for you to get yourself out of it than to come over to our cottage at Thousand Island Park, and sit on the veranda, and gaze out at the river with your dark eyes, and explain yourself. . . . When I get up [there] I shall follow poor dear old Walt Whitman's recipe and "lofe and invite my soul" - and you[.][78]

In early July Holley joined the Carletons at their place at the Thousand Islands while work on the house commenced, but soon she was back again to supervise the building of her new home. She was unable to write, even letters, because she was still weary from illness and the strain of her uncle's death. In August she went back to the Thousand Islands, staying at the Crossman House, trying to write, working in the mornings and spending the afternoons on the riverbank. In early September she surrendered to her need to be at home and returned to the farmhouse as the construction of the mansion went forward.

5

BONNIE VIEW AND MAY

On the look of an unmarried woman: "They do have a sort of a one-sided look, I'll admit, and sort o'curious at certain times, such as processions and et cetery. But . . . in my opinion, there ain't no lonesomeness to be compared to the lonesomeness of the empty-headed and aimless, and no amount of husbands can make up to any woman for the loss of her self-respect."

—Marietta Holley, "Melankton Spicerses Wife"

As the house took form, Holley continued to manage the property from her room in the old cottage. That autumn she hired young Lew Hoxie from Mannsville to be her all-around handyman. He was an eager, ambitious man of eighteen. He accepted her offer of eighteen dollars a month plus board and agreed to work there until spring, but he remained for the next seventeen years. His first duties were as coachman, gardener, and occasional cook. It was sometimes difficult to keep a maid, and Lew took on bits of the housework too, generally making himself indispensable. His life there was busy, with "not much time for mischief," although he admitted "I was a trial at times."[1] When work didn't go just as she wanted it to, Holley would mutter, "Eighteen dollars a month and nothing done!" The specter of penury still haunted the homestead, and Holley was as "clost-fisted" as Josiah in small economies. She wrote lists and messages on scrap paper cut into note-size pieces. She watched the construction of the house for evidence of waste or overspending, to the point of insisting that she couldn't afford French doors for the conservatory that she was having built in the mansion.[2]

Although it has been described as a monument to Victorian ugliness, the fifteen-room house was really a modest version of Queen Anne architecture.[3] The form was exuberant, almost whimsical, a celebration of her wealth and newly realized power. Its three stories surged upward in a metaphor of aspiration, a startling contrast to the plain low farmhouses around the countryside. Holley's friends in the area were quick to point out that her house was not as extravagant as some of the elegant homes in Adams, but many of the rural folk were equally quick to criticize the mansion. The house was a restrained mix of textures and shapes: peaked dormers and gables, ornamental clapboard and spindlework. Wooden lathework, incised and chamfered, laced the gables with elaborate detailing. Embroidery of woodwork spun of simple materials was used with moderation and good taste. The house was full of windows, characteristically tall, thin, and evenly spaced, for light and fresh air. The irregularity of the mansion's shape made its spaces flexible, allowing for additions and modifications, although Holley had no notion in 1888 that her life would require a change. The new house satisfied her: although she had chosen to live among her own country folk, the house identified her as one of the local elite. The mansion demonstrated that she truly had succeeded in making money by her pen, but at the same time it declared that whatever fame she achieved, she would never be one of the gentry. As she had always known, and as Samantha said, the value of a person is not who she is but what she is. Holley, even in abandoning her father's humble house, claimed her birthright as a North Country woman, and she never relinquished that claim.

After the centennial many Americans had begun a search for ancestors and regal lineage to link themselves to the very aristocracy that their democracy had disdained.[4] Even Whittier had inquired whether Holley was related to one Hon. Myron Holley, and her reply was typically disinterested: "I wish I could say I was related to your friend, but I do not know that I am, although Myron is a family name."[5] Some members of her family tried to prove that the Taber line could be traced back to an English title and coat of arms; others claimed that the Holley family stretched back to an Earl of Southworth or to the English astronomer Halley. Marietta was dubious, avowing that "even if it were true, the plain title of American citizen suits me very well."[6] More specifically, she preferred to be a citizen of Jefferson County where "there is so much sanity in the people."

In November the house was finished so that Marietta, Finy, and Lew could move in by Thanksgiving. The lower level of the house had double parlors and a dining room for entertaining, a large kitchen, and a small pantry. At the rear, on the south side, was Holley's conservatory, a room enclosed on two sides by high, arched windows that afforded a view across the clover meadow. The interiors on this first floor were lavishly finished in pale woods, predominantly tulipwood.[7] On the second floor was a suite of four private rooms for Marietta. The large front room on the west side was her study. The room filled the bowed front of the house, and six tall windows caught the sun as the day progressed. Connected to her writing room by a curtained doorway was her bedroom. From either space she could see the gardens, the homes of her neighbors and nearby kin, and Lake Ontario in the distance. Every morning she rose at seven, dressed herself and put up her hair. Breakfast was brought to her in Summer Land, as she called her rooms. She did not want to see anyone or speak with anyone before she set to work.

She had adopted habits to help her maintain her discipline. *Samantha at Saratoga* was a best-seller, and she needed to follow up that success with another to keep her estate and fortune up. If the mood was right, she would sit at her little slant-topped desk and draft a whole story in the morning hours before the one o'clock dinner. When she was composing, she needed to be entirely alone. As she wrote, she would laugh or cry with her characters, believing that if their trials and antics could touch her so deeply, they would not fail to move her readers. Even after she had gone downstairs to lunch, she would carry a notepad and pencil about with her, jotting ideas, names, images, anything that would work in a story. Occasionally she would hurry back up to her study and remain for several hours while the other occupants of the house went about the tasks that they were assigned on her daily list of work to be done.

If anything disturbed or interrupted her, she could not work at all.[8] The study was a haven above the bustle of the household. In it she placed the things she loved best. The mantel of the green-tiled fireplace was covered with a favorite fringed lambrequin. An organ stood against the back wall, its top laden with treasured objects: a pair of fluted vases, two small Venetian statues, photographs of her friends displayed on ornate standards, a hand-painted oil lamp, and a glass bowl filled with flowers. Along the other side of the room stretched a large table littered with books, more pictures, a bejewelled brass lamp, and a rose bowl. These upper rooms were made somewhat soundproof by laying Indian and Persian rugs on top of tinted carpets. Besides the noise of a busy home, there was music. The house could be filled with it. Below in the parlors there were two pianos and another organ. However, for the idle times, books flooded the house, stored in glass-doored cases, on open shelves, even stacked haphazardly on footstools and side tables.[9] The windows were festooned with lace curtains tied back to admit as much sunlight as possible. The stained glass panels were colored soft greens, yellows, and pinks to give the rooms a delicate glow. Wicker furniture and caned chairs suggested the atmosphere of light and air that Holley sought. Her rooms were not furnished for anyone but herself. There was in them none of the sense of display and acquisitiveness so typical of much Victorian interior decoration.[10]

Secure in her new home, Holley watched as her father's cottage was torn down. The garden was enlarged, but a hedge of lilacs, golden alder, and flowering shrubs was planted to separate the flower gardens from the vegetable patch—as if to separate the distinct aspects of her life. When she had returned permanently to her land, she brought back to it a love of beauty and display acquired in her travels. She lavished care and money on plantings for the grounds. Marietta and Lew laid out pathways and flower beds, most of which were in the style of formal English gardens, all edged with chives. There were beds of quaint old-fashioned flowers—poppies, lilies of the valley, forget-me-nots and roses—as well as specimen gardens where she grew exotic shrubs and flowers. The Rose Walk led from an arched-lattice summerhouse covered with floribunda roses and Virginia creeper, through the pasture where the Jersey cow Daisy grazed, to the "liberty pole" where Holley flew Old Glory. Ivy Path led away from the house, along a walk bordered with English ivy, sweet pea, and scarlet runner clambering over the fence to an octagonal gazebo on the north side of the house. This spindlework-and-lattice retreat was eventually grown over with trumpet vine, clematis, and more roses, and it was a fine place for Holley to write or ponder in the heat of summer. The magnificent display, unlike anything else in the rugged North Country, attracted flower fanciers from all over, even luring sightseers and garden clubs from Canada to Holley's glorious gardens.

Rejecting friends' suggestions for names that were too fanciful or pretentious, she chose to call her estate Bonnie View.[11] She always preferred that her name be kept out of the public eye. In fact, when a neighbor adopted the name Holley Park for his farm several years later, using her name rather than his own, she became incensed at his trading on her fame.[12]

The Carletons had remained in the region after the summer season ended to visit Holley's new home while Will gave an occasional lecture or reading. Although he had not written anything that topped the popularity of his *Farm Ballads*, he still drew enormous crowds. An audience of six thousand had attended his second engagement at Thousand Island Park that summer, and when he performed in nearby

Bonnie View, circa 1900.

towns in the North Country, farmers walked ten miles to pay twenty-five or fifty cents to hear Carleton.[13] Marietta was happy for her friend's success and eager to entertain him and his family, but they had to delay their visit. Soon after she moved in, she had been stricken with another severe cold, which rapidly became acute bronchitis.[14] The trauma of the move and fright of her illness produced new material for Samantha, however. With the mild spring, Marietta's health improved enough to permit her to write an account of Samantha and Josiah moving into a new house and the pneumonia that Samantha suffers because of Josiah's hardheadedness and ineptitude. "Josiah's Alarm" was published in *Lippincott's* magazine and in 1893 became a title story for that publisher's two-story collection. The sequence is typical of how Holley relied more and more on the real events in her life for the material spun by Samantha, thereby imparting a special liveliness to it. The Saratoga book had been a best-seller in 1887 partly because the details were so precise, the mood evoked so vividly. Her later works likewise have their genesis in her experience. She gave up writing the sentimental story almost entirely and turned to recreating her realities as Samantha saw them. Frequently she gave the history of a story, claiming that it had come from certain impeccably honest sources.

> Such news had come to us, and come very straight and direct. Miss Deacon Elikum Peck told she that wuz Hetty Avery, and she that wuz Hetty told old Miss Blodgett, and she told the editor of the Au-

Marietta Holley in her study at Bonnie View.

> gerses wife, and she told Miss Preserved Green, and she told Tirzah Ann. It come straight.[15]

In such a litany there is an obvious swipe at country gossips, but there is also a hint at one convention that the sentimental writers used: citing authorities for their fictions as though to absolve themselves of the charge that their works were tainted and trifling. The domestic-sentimental novelists had disguised their stories as diaries, memoirs, journals, and eyewitness accounts to validate them.[16] Samantha established the authenticity of a story by tracing it to its source. In a wonderful irony, that source was most often what Holley actually saw around her in southern Jefferson County.

Bonnie View finally gave her a suitable place to entertain the many persons with whom she had become acquainted in her travels. At fifty-four she was weary of living in others' rooms. With her own grand place, she could be mistress of the manor. A parade of visitors began to come to Bonnie View. When guests were due Holley would send the coach to the train station and have them brought up the long gravel drive, past the birch trees, which she called the grey ladies, to the doorstep. The first to come were Frank and Walter Bliss, president and secretary of the American Publishing Company.[17] The next week Will Carleton and his wife made their first visit. Will was so taken with the grounds that he declared, half in jest, that the macadam highway running along the west side of the property should be renamed Garden Road, and so it was. Soon after, the weekly news began appearing under the heading "Garden Road," then "Bonnie View and Vicinity." Holley was furious that the paper would presume to use the names, especially because she was then in New York City and had not been asked for her permission, although eventually she relented, and the "Garden Road" column continued.

Holley again declined invitations to visit away from home, but no longer out of fear. During the winter of 1890 she stayed entirely at Bonnie View. It was an unusually mild, open winter in the North Country. The sleighing was good. Icehouses were just full enough. Marietta celebrated Christmas by giving gifts to all the children in the neighborhood. She spent the winter quietly doing research and some writing. The previous October, Frances Willard had written asking Holley to prepare "an article on any subject . . . of any length" for the *Union Signal*.

> This paper sends out from 65 to 75 thousand copies per week to all parts of the world, and is the most representative of any now published by women. We pay moderately for contributions from distinguished men and women, and are desirous of one from you at the earliest possible date.

The letter was signed "With high esteem and sincere regard, Your friend and sister, Frances Willard."[18] The tone is more reserved than in the missives of the earlier years, perhaps because the women had met and found that they were allies but not particular friends. Theirs was a political and professional acquaintanceship, not an intimacy. The letter that follows Willard's was written by her sister Mary B. Willard, negotiating for a monthly essay in the style of Betsey Bobbet.[19]

Marietta was deluged with requests of every kind for letters of introduction, dedication poems, Samantha's recipes, legal advice, and editorial comment on unpublished manuscripts.[20] She was usually encouraging to young writers, and her advice to them was specific: take from your long manuscript the parts you think are best and try to get them published as short stories. Seeing one's work in print would enable the writer to spot the defects missed before. Furthermore, "perseverance is the price of success. If a story comes back from an editor, . . . send it to another," twenty times, if necessary.[21] It seems to be odd advice from a writer whose own work had been so quickly accepted and sought after.

Holley's writing was going slowly but well. A collection of her stories from *Peterson's* magazine was published by Lupton under the title *Widder Doodle's Courtship*. In February a winter rainbow seemed to promise her continuing success and satisfaction. Local sentiment regarding woman's rights was increasingly profeminist. The local debating club replaced one of its usual literary evenings with a debate that concluded with the resolution "that a collegiate education is as necessary for a lady as for a gentleman."[22] It was a small victory, but a signal one in which Holley shared. In April Mrs. Newman arrived at Bonnie View to spend several days with Marietta before joining "St. John" at the National Methodist Conference.[23] Holley had finished her novel about the refusal of the 1880 Methodist Conference to seat women delegates. Four duly elected delegates attempted to attend the May general conference in New York City, but their admission was protested, debated, and finally denied. Holley's angry response was *Samantha Among the Brethren,* which was published first in the *Voice* and then as a book by Funk and Wagnalls. The book's dedication is to "All Women, who work trying to bring into dark lives the brightness and hope of a better country." The preface is briefer than usual, full of high moral purpose, but with less humor than before. Most significantly, it was signed "Josiah Allen's Wife, Bonny View, near Adams, New York."[24] Any attempt at masquerade was over. Holley had emerged in Samantha: the identification between writer and persona was complete. Having returned to the source of her inspiration and power, Marietta quietly admitted that she and Samantha were one, that the garrulous country wife was her "second self."[25]

The church had failed Holley in not supporting the woman's rights position. With the information provided by the Newmans from within the church hierarchy, she attacked the prevailing institution's position that women were inferior. Naturally Josiah is against having women sit at the conference. Samantha reasonably argues their right and responsibility to do so. There is a negligible romantic subplot about a spinster and a missionary who postpone their marriage, almost losing each other, to be faithful to their religious commitments. The strength of the work is in Josiah's wrongheaded interpretation of

Scripture while Samantha uses all three of the feminist arguments to circumvent or explain the difficulties in biblical texts that excluded women. She suggests that there may be an error in translation or that the context within which the Scripture had been written rendered the literal meaning irrelevant to modern times. Finally, she insists that the writer, Saint Paul, for example, was just a man expressing his own private opinion. Bolstered by H. W. Beecher's preaching against a literal interpretation of the Bible, Samantha (and Marietta) argue down the issue of plenary inspiration that Josiah espoused.[26] The work is most powerful when Samantha shows the women of a parish keeping alive the church that the long-winded deacons would talk to death. Holley translated her years of experience in her own and neighboring churches into the images for the book. Women organized annual donation parties to support the clergy; women and girls scrimped to buy bits of material to make items to sell at the church bazaars; and it was the women who stripped, scrubbed, papered, and painted the church when it needed to be refurbished. Augusta Wiggins, the Episcopal deaconess in Saratoga, had also given Holley insight into the status of women in that church as well as crucial information about the vigorous missionary work that women did. The book touches on other church-related questions too: the validity of Christian Science, spiritualism, and Adventism. The bitter truth that Samantha settles on is that, regardless of sect, women are excluded. *Samantha Among the Brethren* is angry, sad, cynical and yet comical. Samantha is less in love with Josiah, less patient and tolerant, although she protests otherwise. Her "megumness" is sorely tested. Holley had been drawing for too long on the optimism of the suffragist movement. The arguments and her patience were worn thin.

When the Newmans returned to New York City, Marietta went with them, checking in as usual at the Murray Hill Hotel.[27] Will Carleton and his wife spent time with her there. She was invited out to dine with Mrs. U. S. Grant. Frank Bliss took her to see Buffalo Bill Cody. The change was restful, and she returned home after five weeks in good health and spirits.

Thus began a pattern that lasted through the next two decades. Each spring, usually in late May, Marietta would go into New York City for a few weeks, a month at most, to transact whatever business she needed to and visit her old acquaintances. Otherwise she was occupied at home with her writing, her charities, and her gardens. With increasing frequency trains and carriages brought visitors to her. Mrs. Flack and her daughter came to stay a week. The Carletons brought along Will's mother and sister-in-law for a short visit. Journalists arrived to interview Josiah Allen's Wife in her quiet country home. Long-lost relatives who wanted to claim kinship made the trip, as did fans. Mabel Wagnalls was visiting at Bonnie View one day when a couple of "funereal-looking women" asked to see Samantha.

> They saw her, and looked at her, and continued to look, but spoke no word other than "Good morning." They were seated in the parlor and Miss Holley started off upon a lonely conversation. She talked of the weather and the crops and the church; worked around to quince-canning, and talked some of the bantam hens, the wickedness of gambling, and the prevalence of croup among children. Then I played a piece on the piano, after which Miss Holley began another fine string of general subjects; but still they stayed! So I played another piece and Miss Holley again conversed, but this time with new courage and the glow of inspiration on her face. She spoke of a peculiar flower on her front porch—wouldn't they like to see it? She led them onto the porch and I stationed myself in the doorway. But still they stayed! . . . Miss Holley, with infinite tact and patience, piloted them to an urn of flowers halfway between the house and gate. Here again they paused for a new view of the house, a backward turn that filled us with alarm. But Miss Holley remained firm in her course: she was steering toward the gate and we finally landed there, when one of the women spoke up: "Would you mind showing us over the garden?" Miss Holley felt that duty demanded no more so she excused herself and allowed them to pursue their tour of the garden alone.[28]

The mute admiration that brought such people to Holley's dooryard was welcome testimony to her impact on the lives of women. Visitors were always welcomed when she was at home, and she publicly regretted that some might call to see her and find Samantha not there to greet them. She insisted that whenever she was at Bonnie View, the latchstring was always out.[29]Toward the end of 1890 Holley began soliciting information from her friends on the race problem. Her trips through the Virginia countryside had generated some notions about the difficulties of Negro suffrage that had percolated during the intervening years. As senator Henry Blair had done when Holley needed information regarding temperance, Frances Willard sent her references and sources to study, suggesting that Holley look into Wendell Phillips' speeches as well as "Nicholas Blood" and "Our Brother In Black." Willard scrawled a final comment, "I wish you'd tackle Bellamy's Heaven—that would sell like honey-comb too—lots of good."[30] Holley might have considered such an undertaking, but a utopian novel such as *Looking Backward* would never suit Samantha. Even *Samantha on the Race Problem* was a work she resisted writing. Some time before, two clergymen had called on her at Bonnie View and asked her to write a book on the problems of black suffrage. They came and went unknown to each other. The first was a noted Baptist minister from the South. Two days later, a minister from an eastern city approached her with the same request. Holley stalled, eager to tackle the subject because of her concern with the failure of the abolitionist vision, yet frightened by her lack of firsthand knowledge.

> The earnestness and insistence of these two men, and their coming to me from such different directions at nearly the same time, could not fail to impress me, and I kept thinking about it, and wondering if it really were my duty to try and write this book, and if I did, would it do any good.[31]

By the next Sunday she had become obsessed with the dilemma. She opened her Bible as usual to seek guidance. Holding the book in her left hand, she opened it to a random chapter with her right hand. Closing her eyes, she ran her right thumb along a page until it rested on this passage from Acts 8:26–29: "And the angel of the Lord spake unto Philip saying 'Arise and go toward the South. And he arose and went, and behold a man of Ethiopia—and the spirit said unto Philip go near and join thyself unto this chariot.'" Doubting, Holley tried again, asking aloud if it could be a message for her. The next verse she fingered was Matthew 14:27, "It is I, be not afraid." Making a bargain with herself, she allowed that if she found anything like that a third time, she would take it as a sign. The final experiment yielded this out of Daniel 9:12: "Fear not, Daniel, for from the first day thou didst set thy heart to understand, thy words were heard and I have come for thy words."With such a faith as hers, there could be no retreat. She began at once to write, having a vision as she wrote of the death of Victor, which occurs at the conclusion of the finished work. Like Harriet Beecher Stowe, who received her inspiration for Uncle Tom while in church and claimed that God wrote *Uncle Tom's Cabin,*[32] Holley found herself writing a book as though guided by someone else. Advocating a view that she had never before held—the return of blacks to colonies in Africa—she felt driven to write it all down "by a stronger power than myself." When the manuscript was finished, she doubted the validity of her vision and turned again to the Scriptures. Using her usual method, she came upon this confirmation from Jeremiah 31:15–17

"Now the word of the Lord came to Jeremiah saying 'Go and speak to . . . the Ethiopian, saying I will deliver thee in that day.'"[33] She was convinced.

In May 1892 Holley was invited to Omaha to a reception for the bishops, delegates, and friends of the General Conference of the Methodist Episcopal Church. The invitation arrived through the courtesy of Mrs. Newman with a delegate's card included. Holley's views presented in *Samantha Among the Brethren* made her an eagerly sought guest, but she refused the invitation. Her health had been poor since she had weathered an attack of grippe that winter in New York City, and the "pen paralysis" that thwarted her urge to write was beginning to plague her. She composed in longhand, copying and recopying her drafts because she felt that an amanuensis simply would not get the dialect right. The final draft of *Samantha on the Race Problem* was at the publishers by the end of May, and Holley needed a rest. She did not even go into New York City to confer with Frank Dodd on her work but had him visit her at Bonnie View.[34] She had finally achieved sufficient success so that she no longer needed to write for subsistence. Her continuing commitment was to reform, using her writing "to accomplish all the good [I] can while [I] have health and strength."[35] *Samantha on the Race Problem* was just such an attempt at presenting workable reforms despite her increasing physical disabilities.

Samantha's trials in the "southern states" were precipitated by the illness of Josiah's son, Thomas Jefferson, and his wife and daughter after they had taken up residence on a southern plantation. Samantha's keen vision of the situations that surround her retains its rustic northern bias. She renders it with reasonableness and restraint that contrast with the ranting, pious oratory of reformers whom she meets along the way. Before beginning their mission south, Samantha characteristically describes the homely events around Jonesville, and in doing so gives the reader examples of other disenfranchised, enslaved members of the great democracy. There is in Jonesville a young boy who has been put in bondage to a miserable, cruel deacon. There are factories in nearby cities where industrial workers are reduced to the condition of slaves by the economic complex, and runaways from the system become street beggars. Finally there are women who, with no vote, cannot break their own chains much less anyone else's. These captives compare implicitly with the black characters she encounters in the South who are equally enslaved in spite of their legal freedom. The novel begins with a vigorous but abstract sermon by Josiah's cousin, John Richard, a colporteur who preaches colonization for the freed Negroes. Samantha rarely soars into eloquence in this book, depending instead on well-developed, concrete stories of slaves, freedmen, and landowners. Midway through the work, Samantha recants her earlier position on the race problem in a typically honest admission:

> For a time after I went South things looked so new and strange to me, and my daughter Maggie was so firm in her belief, that I seemed to think just as she did. . . . And I guess I even outdone her in drawin' metafors, and drawin' 'em out to great distances, as my way is.
>
> For I am always one to speak out and tell how things look to me today; if they look different tomorrow under the light of some different knowledge, why, then I'll speak out agin and tell that when the time comes.[36]

Samantha's first solution is to give the ballot to white women in the South and such black women as can meet a standard of intelligence (presumably reading, writing, and religion). After considerable speculation and talk with the Negro Victor, Samantha changes her mind.

> I see jest how it wuz; I see that nobody, no matter how strong you should fix the medicine and how powerful the doses you might give, could cure this distemper, this instinctive, deep-rooted feelin' of antipathy and repulsion towards the negro.
>
> I see that no amount of pills and plasters wuz a goin' to make the negro feel free and easy with the white race.
>
> . . . any amount of flowery speeches or proclamations, or enactments, or anything, hain't a goin' to amalgamate the two races and make 'em blend into another and be a hull one.[37]

For Samantha, as well as for Holley, it was a dramatic shift in belief, a conversion.

Although it is dated by its subject matter, this book stands as one of Holley's best ones even now. The sketches of Negro life on and off the plantations, the images of a variety of black experience and types, and the re-creations of the "darky" dialect are some of Holley's most skillful writing. Furthermore, she had constructed a novel, not merely a travelogue. Perhaps because her vision of the book began with the end—Victor's death—the work has architecture, with a new balance in image and character that is absent in the other novels. At the same time, while Samantha's voice remains consistent, other voices and dialects are heard. Some of the material is old stuff like suffrage, the innocence of children, and the importance of faith; but much is fresh and vital in the book. Holley was writing out of a new source, having tapped a new well of feeling.

Meanwhile some of the old pieces were being republished. Lupton again arranged to collect several of the stories from *Peterson's* magazine into a single volume. Her popularity swelled. The list of visitors to Bonnie View increased weekly. Invitations to appear or speak flooded in. In November she was invited to read in New York City on a program with Charles Dudley Warner, Edward Eggleston, Will Carleton, Marion Harland and others, but she chose not to.[38] Being on a rostrum was

> something like mounting the pile of faggots to be offered up. . . . I always wanted a comfortable place in the shadows where I could look out . . . and listen with delight. It is something like my feeling for deep water. I was always afraid of any personal excursion, but I loved to sit on the shore and see divers of my sex disporting themselves among the waves.[39]

That same week she was unanimously chosen by the American Association of Authors, of which Carleton was president, to serve as the vice-president representing New York State.[40] Barton, Stowe, Mrs. H. W. Beecher, Elizabeth Stuart Phelps, Willard, and others asked Holley to use her influence to advocate improvement in women's dress, changes that would encourage freedom and health, such as abandoning corsets, high-heeled shoes, and long-trained dresses that trailed in the street.[41] Holley was invited to sit on the committee on literature and art for the Columbian Exposition at Chicago, but her attention was entirely directed at the book about the world's fair that she was writing for Funk and Wagnalls.[42]

The Reverend Mr. Funk of Funk and Wagnalls had asked during a visit in October 1890 that she write three more books for the firm, one of which was to be about Samantha's attending the world's fair. When he asked her to set a price for that book, she stipulated fourteen thousand dollars, and he agreed. The terms were set, a deadline arranged, and maps and guidebooks sent to Bonnie View. There was a rush to get the book out while the exposition was still fresh in everyone's mind, so she set to work at once.[43] As she wrote, the pain in her right hand increased and spread to her arm. It seemed to be more than writer's cramp or pen paralysis. Very likely it was either the result of a pinched nerve from the fall she'd taken in 1883 or carpal tunnel syndrome. She found that by limiting herself to shorter periods of work she could keep the pain to a minimum, but Funk's deadline pressed on her until she forced herself to continue writing in spite of the pain. The worry over whether she could work or not made her ill, and she wrote to Funk asking to be released from the contract. He replied firmly that the company would hold her to the terms. Holley's physician then wrote Funk saying that her health was in jeopardy because of her anxiety. Funk relented somewhat, and it was agreed that she would do the best she could. Driven by her sense of duty, she wrote for too long. One morning in the first week of April 1893, she struggled with her pen until the pain became so acute that it engulfed her. Frightened, she fled her study to walk under the budding maples—and to pray. There seemed to be no way out. She could not dictate her manuscripts because she could not bear to have anyone near when she composed. The axiom "better pain than paralysis" was empty for her.[44]

In despair she abandoned the writing for awhile. Within days a letter arrived from a clergyman in Pennsylvania who was himself an author. It was essentially a fan letter, but in it he suggested that she try a new mode of composing that he had found useful: dictating into a graphophone and having a typist make a copy from the recording. Holley sent Lew into Watertown to buy a typewriter and graphophone. Lew set about learning to type immediately. In private, Holley sketched a rough outline and dictated onto the disk, then gave the recording to Lew for transcription. The method worked, and *Samantha at the World's Fair* was finished on schedule. Eventually she abandoned the recording step as too costly, but the graphophone so pleased her that she wrote to Clara suggesting that she might find it useful. Clara dictated the first letter to Marietta, thanking her but expressing discomfort with the scheme and surprise at her voice sounding "like some grim old croaker with a *horrible* cold."[45] It is likely that such distortion along with Marietta's lisp made recording difficult as well as expensive. After she and Lew had done another book together, Lew became adept enough at reading her huge scrawled script that he could type directly from her draft copy. To most people, her handwriting was simply illegible, much like Samantha's "duck's tracks." Frances Willard even missed a luncheon appointment with her in New York City simply because she could not read the message.[46] Much of Holley's handwriting during and after this period is nearly indecipherable. The pain wearied her; consequently, the writing in *Samantha at the World's Fair* is decidedly less vigorous and fresh than it was in the foregoing works.

Dedicated to "Columbia—who has just sailed out and discovered woman. And to the sect discovered—," the book focuses on women's issues and temperance much as the previous works had done. Samantha sees in small domestic events, scenes at the exposition, and trials of travel more opportunities for arguing the old issues. Much of the material is recycled from previous works. In fact, Samantha sometimes pauses to recollect and reflect on situations in the earlier books giving enough background information so that someone who had not read the first book would still get her point and perhaps seek out the original work. There are two passages in this volume that demonstrate again how closely Holley's life and Samantha's experiences are linked. Early in the book, Samantha recounts the story of a brother and sister with equal talents and ambitions. When the parents need care, the girl is required to surrender her intentions and stay at home while the boy goes into the world to make his fortune. It is a position the girl accepts as inevitable, even natural, but a posture that cripples. The book ends with her marriage to a proper gentleman after her parents' deaths, but the intervening years are hollow and unsatisfying, much as some of Holley's earlier years had seemed. Further along in the book, as an example of the curse of drink, Samantha tells the story of a drunkard who murders a little girl who is then chased through swamp and woods by the enraged townsmen. The account is a precise rendering of a vicious murder committed near Pierrepont Manor a few years before. As Samantha says:

> How true it is that, from the Bible down to Josiah Allen's Wife, you have got to talk in stories in order to impress the masses! You have to hold up the hammer of personal incident to drive home the nail of Truth and have it clench and hold fast.[47]

Holley did not go far for her stories. The most marked change in this novel is in the Allen's marriage. Samantha and Josiah argue cuttingly on this trip. The barbed remarks more often hit a tender nerve rather than a heart armored by principle and Christian tolerance. Although *Samantha at the World's Fair* ends with a wedding, Samantha's concluding remarks confirm Holley's sensitivity to the lie within the convention.

> How different, how different Josiah Allen and I look at things! And still we workship each other—jest about.[48]

Samantha at the World's Fair was scheduled for publication in September. Marietta was at the Thousand Islands resting. In late August a letter arrived from Clara Barton postmarked Alexandria Bay, New York. She and George Pullman, "Brother George," were guests of the elder brother of all the Pullmans, camping while they worked on correspondence and reports. Gleefully Clara anticipated seeing Marietta again, slipping into Samantha's speech patterns: "You see I have waived all ceremony. I don't even wait for an over-skirt. I only wonder that in my delight I have not gone off in poetness."[49] The two women and George made a joyful trio. To Clara Marietta could tell everything, sharing the most dangerous and delightful feelings. She was the only person to whom Marietta spoke of life with Sylphina. The friends no doubt regretted that much of their life had passed before they met one another and made a pact to live to be a thousand, as if to stretch out their intimacy. Luxuriating in Clara's friendship, Holley was lulled and comforted, but the end of the summer season brought her new pain. Her brother Bright died in Phoenix, Arizona.

A strange occurrence at the time of Bright's death confirmed Marietta's belief in spirit visitation and communication. Sylphina had been resting at Bonnie View in the afternoon when she began to hear rappings in the room opposite hers. Because she was alone in the house, she ignored the sound even though it increased until finally there was a "thundering rap on the headboard above her head." That evening, Marietta and her niece Ella asked the Ouija what the rapping meant and tried automatic writing. Marietta wrote out that it was a warning for her and her sister. A few days later the notice of Bright's death arrived, and she calculated that the rappings had coincided with his passing.[50] A letter from Bright's widow told Marietta the circumstances of his sudden death from pneumonia. Bright had become the Honorable Brightman Holley, probate judge, after leaving Montana. He had built himself a substantial career and reputation, but he left behind no children, no more Holleys.[51]

Marietta put her things in order at Bonnie View and left for New York City to join the Newmans. After a week at the Murray Hill and a jaunt to Saratoga Springs, the party left for Chicago to meet Mrs. grant and the Carletons to attend the closing of the fair. She later reported to the Reverend Mr. Funk that if she had visited the fair first, she never could have written the book. She loathed and feared crowds; they made her "weary and half-sick."[52] On the last day she fell ill with bronchitis and was confined to bed for a week. As she lay abed lonely and ill, she thought she heard fairylike rappings like those she had heard before in her own study and conservatory. Then she had taken them as proof that—as a psychic had promised—she would receive messages from the spirit world. This time,

> instead of filling me with fear, they filled me with content and joy, as if someone was trying to give me comfort and courage. If friends want to come into one's room, they surely rap before entering.[53]

The rest of the group had continued with their trip west, but on their return, Mrs. Newman accompanied Marietta back to Saratoga where she entered Dr. Strong's sanitarium to take sun and electric baths. When she had recovered enough, she went on to New York City to transact some business with her publishers, then returned to Bonnie View.

Holley returned to a household livelier than it had been in some time. There was a new maid in the household, a black woman named Rhoda, who Marietta felt had psychic abilities because the rappings and assorted parapsychological events increased when she came into the house. In addition, there was a child at Bonnie View.

For years it had seemed that Marietta would only have her "thought children," as she called her characters.[54] To another woman writer she wrote a congratulatory note on the emergence of her "mind-child."[55] Later, when she visited the writer at her home, Holley was amazed, wondering "how can she ever write her bright books in this place, for her three pretty children, little flyaways, seemed to be everywhere present. No spot seemed to be exempt from their noisy and riotous presence."[56] Writing and mothering appeared to be incompatible to Holley. Books were peaceful, long-lived progeny. Even Clara Barton recognized that the books were a substitute for a brood of offspring. In a letter praising *Samantha at the World's Fair,* Clara exclaimed: "What treasures your 11 children are; what a family to sit honoringly on your shelves, and look lovingly upon you, as you create for them still another companion."[57]

For Holley the opportunity for motherhood came late, when she was fifty-eight, and it arrived askew. May Shaver, who was eight years old at this time, was the daughter of Will Shaver, the subscription agent for Holley's book *My Wayward Pardner*. He had been living a checkered career since then, picking up odd jobs around the area and getting into minor scrapes. The previous year he had been arrested for assaulting a man during an argument. He had a boisterous temperament that was made more so by drink. Another arrest for being drunk and disorderly followed when he stoned the home of a young woman in Adams.[58] He was clearly no kind of parent for a young girl, and because there appeared to be no mother around, Holley took the girl in, much as she had taken up stray boys. With May, things were to be quite different.

From the first, Marietta treated her like a daughter. She wanted her dressed and educated properly. During the winter of 1893 May attended the district school with moderate academic success, and Holley's involvement in the school became intense. In the previous years, she had given each child a little gift at the end of first term, but beginning in 1893 she gave prizes to students who had attained the best grades and deportment.[59] Holley began giving parties for the little girls in the neighborhood. In spring and summer the servant would lay out dainty picnics on the lawn or in the gardens. There were immaculate white linens spread on the grass and little striped stools for the girls to sit on.[60] Often the visitors to Bonnie View were women who brought with them their daughters, nieces, or granddaughters to play with May. Holley took fewer trips away from home, and those she did make were shorter. The presence of little May in the house made it a happier place and—in spite of her continuing pain—Marietta produced seven hundred pages of manuscript over the winter of 1893–94. In February she left for New York City to see the Newmans off as they sailed for Europe, but she hurried back to Bonnie View afterward, stopping only to do some business.[61]

That spring Holley was stricken again with a respiratory infection, but she continued to work excitedly on creating a home for her family. She and Lew set out sixty or so new trees: evergreens, fruit trees, and mountain ash. The grounds began to flourish again in the mild summer. Holley stayed away from the little "snuggery" on the third floor of the house where she had resorted to going to draft her manuscripts.[62] A child in the house had made such a retreat necessary. Motherhood, even surrogate motherhood, is "a condition of life which perhaps, except in the case of the strongest-minded, blurs the sharp sight and weakens the firm grasp" that writing requires.[63] She wrote less frequently and without much enthusiasm. Lippincott published her two-story collection *Josiah's Alarm and Abel Perry's Funeral*, but neither piece was new. She was preoccupied with May and Bonnie View.

The circumference of her world diminished. The persons she saw were old friends and a few people in nearby villages whom she and May would visit: the rector in Pierrepont Manor, the Fords in Mannsville, a woman friend in Watertown. Then in late May Holley bought the cedar swamp across the road, two acres that lay downhill toward the west.[64] With a passion she directed Lew and assorted workmen in tearing out trees and hacking back underbrush. She ensured that no wolves would lurk there again. The ground was drained, ponds dug, and rivulets deepened to create a place for flowers and shrubs to flourish. A summerhouse was built at the end of a series of pathways with arched bridges that spanned the little streams. In her zeal for improvements, she had a stream diverted to run through the henhouse to keep it clean. So proud was she of her flock of chickens that when the editor of the Des Moines *Mail and Times* mentioned them during an interview, she trooped twelve peeping chicks into the parlor to show them off.[65]

Holley and Lew worked through the summer; she directed what should be planted or dug, and he did it. At the same time a horde of visitors demanded her attention, sometimes as many as fifteen in one week. In August she went off to the Thousand Islands for four weeks to spend time with Clara Barton and George Pullman again. The Queen and Brother George took Marietta on a tour of the islands, her first, and she repaid them with a visit to Bonnie View.[66] Clara was a great lover of roses and lilacs. The gardens and park delighted her, as did the conservatory, which Marietta was having enlarged. Clara was so taken with one area of the rose garden that she claimed it, and it was dubbed Clara's Bower. As usual, Clara's visit was brief, but even in so short a time as a week she and May formed a deep affection. May was wild, a bit of a rascal, but she was a loving child. Like Marietta's flowers, she bloomed.

With autumn session beginning, May returned to her studies, and Marietta tried to write. She managed a few essays and stories, but there was little new material. Her correspondence with Clara continued, Marietta often expressing concern for the older woman's health and safety, Clara usually allaying those fears and complaining about the state the Red Cross organization was in. The winter lasted late into 1895, with an Easter storm in April that kept many from church. Holley left home for her annual spring trip into New York City, where she spent time with the Carletons, Rose Cleveland, and Barton and Pullman. She continued to stay at the Murray Hill, even though Clara preferred the Waldorf and would have liked to have had Holley nearer her.

The friendship with Will Carleton was in flux. Because Will was an accomplished raconteur, they traded stories. He even declared that she was one of the best storytellers he knew. That contradicted her own image of herself because, like Samantha,

> instead of proceeding methodically with a story from beginning to end,—I was just as liable to begin in the middle and work out to both ends. . . . I had only this in my favor—I never drew out my stories until the English language and my hearers patience were exhausted, but tried to get to the climax of a story before the ending was forgotten.[67]

Carleton had helped Holley by reading her manuscripts and interceding for her with editors and publishers; he often read his poems to her and tried out recitations. He had been her escort and champion in public. From her he demanded absolute loyalty. The first issue of Will's magazine *Everywhere* had appeared the previous autumn. When Holley furnished him with a story each month for *Everywhere,* their relationship assumed another dimension. Then when someone offered her eight times what he was paying her and she accepted, Carleton flew into a rage. He expected her to write exclusively for his magazine, and she refused, just as she refused to allow her picture to be offered as a premium for the magazine. Carleton's anger abated after he stalked out, but the friendship was severely damaged. The relationship with Will had cooled so thoroughly that when his mother died in January 1896, it was Will's wife, not Will, who wrote Marietta about the illness and death. His correspondence with her after this is reserved and clearly businesslike, lacking the easy jocularity of the old days.

Concluding her annual spring visit, Marietta returned from New York City after having breakfast with Will's wife. The school year was ending for May. At the conclusion of the final day, the teacher and all the children were invited to Bonnie View for a gramaphone concert and cake and ice cream on the lawn.[68] Holley wanted May to have the kind of genteel girlhood she had never had, a feast of friends and parties.

May had met Holley's namesake, Marietta Holley Ford, who was nearly her age. The Fords belonged to one of the prominent families in Mannsville that had begun including Holley in their socials when she was a beginning novelist. James Ford and Frannie Minar Ford had cherished their friendship with her. When their daughter had been born in 1878, the new father had written a loving note to their friend: "Betsey . . . has not disappointed her aunt. A fine girl brought us much joy this morning. Mother and child doing *very* nicely. Miss Marietta Holley Ford sends her best respects and winks her eyes knowingly."[69] Having a child named for her had brought Holley immense joy, even then. She would often remark to her niece

Ella Page Copeland that it was sad to be the last of one's family. As her mother had, Marietta wished she had a way to pass on her name and heritage. May Shaver seemed to provide that.

Holley lavished attention on the girl and sought out the best companions for her. When the writer's friends visited at Bonnie View, May was included in the festivities. Mabel Wagnalls and Mrs. Will Carleton visited, but Clara was now too often off on Red Cross business to call at Bonnie View. She longed for the integrated life her friend had. She wanted to rest, writing in her journal that she "would like a quiet country retreat with no one to talk to, and only books to read."[70] To her friend she wrote: "I see the house, the rooms, the books, the . . . grounds, the garden, the fish pond: . . . I wonder if you fully realize what an ideal home and life you have made up for yourself; I have never seen the combination of the two as fully [realized]."[71] Clara had begun construction of her own hermitage in Glen Echo, Maryland, just a few miles from Washington, D.C., so the two women shared their designs for their ideal homes. Their letters are full of domestic details and endearments, with Clara always asking to be remembered to Lew and "the Babe," or May. In September 1895, Marietta had been dangerously ill, too sick even to have Clara visit. In October she sent an aching letter to Clara declaring how disappointed they were—"babe, chickens, ducks, trout, parrot and all"—at not seeing their precious friend. She enclosed a snip of manuscript about the Red Cross, which was included in her forthcoming book *Samantha in Europe*, adding that "a little sharp bit was better than a long tedious account."[72] After her bout with "enteric fever," she had decided that the water system was at fault and so had the place torn up and a new water tank and plumbing installed by "a carnival of plumbers, tinsmiths and carpenters."[73] By Christmas she had heard that Clara was going to Turkey for six to eight months to assist with relief activities after the Armenian massacre. To Holley it was a separation fraught with danger. May's comment on learning of Clara's departure echoed Marietta's fear: "Oh dear, when she comes back she will come with wings."[74] To give her friend something of hers to take up her leisure in the crossing, Marietta sent "my latest child, *Samantha in Europe*."[75]

Her concern with her other child, May, was growing as the girl did. With the contribution of a library and Sunday school papers, Holley organized a Sabbath school in the Grenell schoolhouse. The Methodist minister from Mannsville, the Reverend Mr. Hancock, served as preacher, but Holley was the treasurer and moving force of the Hope Sabbath School. Attendance was much larger than expected at the midafternoon services, so large in fact that sometimes benches had to be set out on the grass in the schoolyard to accommodate the children and adults who came to hear Hancock's sermons. In 1898 special permission was obtained from the Episcopal bishop to allow them to use the Book of Common Prayer for their service, an apparent reversion to the Holley family's Episcopalianism, although Mr. Hancock continued to give the sermon when he was available.[76] When he was not, Mrs. Kincaid, wife of a local rector, gave a sermon instead and was so successful that she was often invited to return to the pulpit, much to Holley's delight. A woman preaching was a sure sign of progress in religious matters.

As concerned as Holley was that May receive a sound Christian education, she also wanted the girl to learn the social amenities. She often had guests to teas, concerts, plays, and lawn parties in the gardens or at the ponds, which had been stocked with perch, bass, and trout. To accommodate the increasing bustle in the household, Marietta was also designing the remodeling of the house itself. Three new rooms were to be added, and the pantry, conservatory, and upper chambers were to be enlarged. Sylphina was to have a sitting room of her own upstairs, and May's room was enlarged with a dressing room added.[77]

By summer's end Holley was exhausted. When district school reopened, she slipped away to the Thousand Islands to rest. Clara had returned from Turkey safely, and she and George Pullman were at the resort working on the report of their trip. The Carletons were also in town, but Holley only dined with them, not staying at their cottage as she had before. Old friends were dropping away slowly. The Newmans were preparing to go to California to live, and they invited Holley to join them in New York City or Saratoga Springs for one last good visit.[78] Marietta announced that she was refusing all invitations to stay home and oversee the construction on the house and be with May. The winter passed quietly once the work on the house was finished. The exotic plants in her conservatory bloomed extravagantly. At Christmas Lew and Marietta went to a protected corner in the rose garden where Lew cleared away the snow so that she could cut the white blooms of her rare Christmas rose, though the flower would not last long after it was taken into the warm conservatory.

May fared better than the Christmas rose. She was an able student, as Holley had been, but she applied herself more methodically, acquitting herself well in her studies of arithmetic, history, physiology, composition, geography, drawing, spelling, penmanship, and reading.[79] Quick and charming, the child was usually a delightful presence in the house. She plainly loved her adopted home and emulated her surrogate mother. When she played house, even with grown-ups, and it was her turn to be the caller, she would make the usual social chatter and then exclaim, "Oh, by the way, I have brought a manuscript with me; would you please read it and give me your advice?" With May's influence the farm became a domestic menagerie with a pug dog named Lassie; a kitten and a cat called Trilby and Dick Swiveller, respectively; a duck named Dr. Quack; the tame doves Barkis and Peggoty; the two turkeys, Lord Baltimore and Queen Elizabeth; and the horses Tom and George as well as the parrot Polly.[80]

Holley's time with May did not keep her from her annual spring trip into New York City. She arranged meetings with her publishers and friends and allowed them to organize parties and visits to mediums for her. Although she was away from the homestead only briefly, she missed the burst of North Country spring. To the astonishment of some neighbors, she had Lew pack up the first of Bonnie View's daffodils and jonquils and send them to her at the Murray Hill. The lure of the city was strong. Going there meant she could see her old friends who were too busy or frail to get to Bonnie View. Clara wrote to her in the spring of 1897 that she would make the trip to New York City from Washington, D.C., during Marietta's time there if she would have "some little snatches of time to give to me for a day or two or three, that I might be able to be near you."[81] By staying a few extra days, Holley managed to spend time with Clara, realizing her desire to "clasp her hand once more and have even one talk."[82] Barton and Pullman dashed up from Washington for a party that was held in Marietta's honor. S. Homer Eaton, a well-known elocutionist from Boston, was recruited to present the character of Samantha at the party. The Wagnalls were part of the entertainment, too, as Mabel sang and the publisher made a genial speech. The evening was a success, but Clara and George's departure the next evening dimmed Holley's delight. She was terribly distressed that Clara was going off to assist the Americans in Cuba. While they were together in New York, she had helped Clara with a piece that she was writing for the *North American Review*."[83] She had not taken a scrap of manuscript with her to work on; in fact, she seemed to be doing little writing of her own.

Samantha in Europe was hailed as the best book of travel since Twain's *Innocents Abroad*.[84] In it Samantha accompanies Martin, a wealthy, villainous American businessman, on a whirlwind European tour, dragging along his son and Josiah. Martin is on the trip merely to be able to say he has been there, to compete with his cohorts. Samantha ridicules his attitude at every turn. She uses the views of the Asian Al Faizi to highlight the differences between the American

The Holley Household. *Left to right*, Rhoda, Lew Hoxie, May, and Holley.

ideal and reality much as she had done with Betsey Bobbet's opinions before. Still there is no doubt that this is a travel book: Samantha pauses for elaborate descriptions of the scenery and her responses to it. Such passages are precise down to the dimensions of parks and monuments, as though Holley had not deviated from the guidebooks she used. The relationship between Josiah and Samantha is mostly submerged, although it sometimes comes up in bitter, strained exchanges. This time Samantha is not out to tout woman's rights or temperance, but to demonstrate her conviction that the serious business of government and industry needs to be humanized, regardless of national or international politics. She concludes that one place is no better or worse than another, only different.

The standard stylized travel-writing that had made Europe accessible to Americans was anachronistic when more and more Americans were themselves traveling to the Continent. Exotic places became more interesting, and Samantha's slant gave the travelogue a new twist. With the success of *Samantha in Europe*, the editor of the *Christian Herald* decided that a world tour book would be a good publishing idea. Dr. Louis Klopsch asked for the book in fifty-two weekly installments and agreed to her price, $100 for each installment. After contracting by telephone to undertake the project, Holley reconsidered. The pressure of a weekly deadline was frightful. Furthermore, DeWitt Talmadge, also an editor at the *Christian Herald* as well as a renowned writer and preacher, was making a world tour while sending back to the paper descriptions of what he saw. Holley feared that her work, done from maps and guidebooks, would suffer by comparison. Klopsch insisted that she honor her agreement; she shrewdly bargained to retain copyright. The work was done, and in 1899 she sold the book rights to Dillingham.[85] This was her first transaction with that firm, which catered to the female audience by publishing writers who would attract it.[86]

Samantha's global excursion is a healing mission. Her grandson Tommy needs a trip abroad to aid his recuperation from measles and a lung ailment. Soon a whole party of characters is organized to go, and Josiah is to be left at the farm. Samantha has become considerably more sophisticated in her travel, enough so that she is embarrassed by Josiah's country ways and rustic nonsense. Samantha has gradually ceased being the Yankee and become more simply a rustic philosopher. She continues to compare whatever wonder she sees to its counterpart back in Jonesville and to find anything American as good as, if not better than, anything foreign. Her position as an alien sharpens Samantha's increasing loneliness, even after Josiah joins them at their California sailing. There is no comfort or connection in his presence:

> What two folks ever did see each other? Why, I never see Josiah, and Josiah never sees me. Not the real us.[87]

More and more Holley's letters sounded like Samantha's "episodin and allegorin." She retreated to her gardens more often, entertaining fewer of her friends and more of May's but writing her homely letters to Clara, who was frequently at her own place in Glen Echo.

> Well while you have been doing the world's work, like the noble woman that you are, I have been jogging along here in the corner, keeping Babe [May] in order, attending to our little sabbath school, entertaining visitors.[88]

But for all her activity at Bonnie View, there was an ineffable loneliness hovering.

> Write me when you can. An inspiration always comes to me with your letters, an inspiration greatly needed by me here tucked away between dairy farms and sheep pastures. . . . I am writing away for dear life when I get a chance. I have just finished a story and have got another one on the docket which I am writing at every chance I get.[89]

Benefits and "sociables" could not make up for Holley's increasing sense of mortality. Her cousin Henry died at his home in the state of Washington in June.[90] Frances Willard had sent a letter asking her to protest to the administration at Princeton University against sanctioning a saloon near the college, but Holley replied that if they had not listened to Moses and the prophets, they would not listen to her.[91] Willard was planning a visit to Bonnie View at last when she suddenly died.[92] A personal note from Willard's partner Anna Gordon consoled Marietta, but later when Gordon invited her to write an "estimate of her life and labors" for a book she was compiling about Willard, Holley recoiled because—as she confided to Clara—she had not known Willard well enough.[93]

Only May seems to have kept Marietta's spirits up. She hired a private tutor for the girl when May needed more than the Giddingsville school could offer.[94] The house was often filled with May's friends as Marietta watched the child who had quickly grown into an adolescent. At thirteen May was vivacious and mischievous. She even scampered into the park to cut down a Christmas tree, a prank that surely shook her surrogate mother's nerves.[95] Marietta often sought out quiet spaces, even when she ventured into New York City. Although she was lonely, her solitude was more than ever necessary. She tried to entice Clara to the Murray Hill: "I have got the quietist little corner where I take my meals—as sheltered and cozy as Bonnie View. We can have a good visit with no one to molest or make afraid."[96] When the summers at Bonnie View were ended, she would take a few weeks along the Saint Lawrence River, after the tourists were gone.

Meanwhile Lew was making a life of his own separate from the family. He had been devoted to Holley since his employment eighteen years before, spending his young manhood doing whatever varied service she requested. The relationship had certainly been mutually beneficial. Lew acquired skills at things like horticulture and typewriting, which he then parlayed into other jobs. His days at Bonnie View acquainted him with graciousness and gentility that he would hardly have known otherwise; but the household of women was too constraining, and Holley's stand on temperance cramped his sporting style. He spent more time away from the estate, often on extended bicycle excursions. Finally he built a house near Sandy Pond, where he and his friends, a gang of rowdy young men, spent weekends.

Clara was at work on her own book about the Red Cross during the winter of 1898–99. Holley missed Barton and her letters, but in December she received a facsimile of her friend's dear face. It was the plaster model of the marble bust which was to be displayed at the Capitol. Holley had sent photographs of Clara to the sculptor so that he could work on it during Clara's absence. She planned to have the bust placed in a velvet case and put on the wall as "a benediction to all who pass beneath."[97]

Clara was struggling along writing her autobiography and sharing bits with her friend, who reassured her of its quality. Writing one's autobiography seemed a terribly significant act. Not only did it remind Holley of her own mortality, but it put her achievements into focus and—in her mind—whittled them down considerably. As she read Clara's life story, her own seemed petty, "so small a point as to make itself nearly invisible."[98] Except for her spring journeys into New York City, she lived a narrow life. When she returned from her 1899 excursion, she brought a twenty-eight-volume set of books for the Sunday school. She had met with Will Carleton, and he had agreed to give a benefit reading for the Hope School, but relations between them were still cool.[99] His letters to her from Brooklyn are restrained and concerned with business, with a token invitation to have an "old-fashioned visit with us," but the old exuberance is not there.[100]

While Clara was in Cuba setting up hospitals and homes for children of the *reconcentrados* (detained revolutionaries), John Newman died.[101] He had called on Marietta at her hotel just before he left for his final trip to Saratoga Springs, where he lived out the last days. Mrs. Newman wrote their friend, describing his final moments and telling her of her plans to plunge into religious work abroad.[102] With renewed vigor, spurred by a sense that she too needed to make a significant contribution, Holley began churning out more short fiction, primarily for the *Christian Herald*, the *Ladies' Home Journal*, and *Everywhere*.

May was quickly developing into a young woman with enthusiasms of her own. Marietta fretted over May but shared her worries only with Clara in their letters and rare talks. She was careful never to speak her innermost fears to anyone other than Clara. In September Marietta's dread of horses was reinforced when May had an accident. She had taken the docile horse and the light cart to Adams with a party of her friends, apparently without Holley's permission. A short way up the road, the cart broke and toppled, trapping the youngsters under the surrey top until a passerby rescued them.[103] There was no serious injury, but clearly May was beginning to show her willful, ungovernable side. The old adage "blood will tell" haunted Marietta, although she still clung to her belief in the inherent rather than inbred qualities of children. As if to insist that her care could overcome any propensities May might have inherited from her father, she began calling the girl "Marietta Holley Shaver," even though no formal adoption or legal change took place. After a summer of Sabbath school activities and ice cream socials, Holley took her two namesake children on a tour of the Thousand Islands and Alexandria Bay. Marietta Holley Ford and Marietta Holley Shaver must have made a pleasant picture trailing after the aged Miss Holley. At the end of that week, she was taken ill and retired to her suite of rooms to be attended by her new physician, Dr. Gross. She had been sick frequently over the past two years and had often been stricken suddenly. She took refuge in the conservatory, where the humid warmth and blooming vista seemed to soothe her. At sixty-four Marietta faced the awareness that May, who was almost fifteen years old, needed a firmer hand than she could or would impose. In the fall of 1900 Marietta sent the girl away to live among the nuns at a Catholic boarding school of excellent reputation in Rome, New York.[104] Only sixty miles away, Saint Peter's School was near enough for visits, and the company of women and girls from good families seemed more important than the emptiness of the big house at Bonnie View.

6

BONNIE VIEW AND BEYOND

The beauty and clamor of life will go on without us. You see, we hain't needed so much as we in our egotism think we are. The world will get along without us, while we rest in peace.

But until then we have got to move along: we can't set down anywhere, and set there. No: if we·want to be fore mothers and fore fathers, we mustn't set still. . . . We must keep movin' on.

—Marietta Holley, *Sweet Cicely*

THE SOLITUDE OF BONNIE VIEW was relieved when May returned for school vacations, sometimes bringing girlfriends from the convent school with her. Then Holley gave elegant parties and planned outings for the young women. Publicly but unofficially, May's name had been changed to Marietta Holley Shaver in Holley's attempt to claim her and leave her own name as legacy. At school the switch might have worked, but back at Bonnie View everyone knew she was still May. She usually participated in the Hope Sabbath School activities, often giving recitations on temperance or suffrage. As a student she seems to have done well under the nuns' tutelage, but she was still prone to unladylike outbursts of mischievous energy.

One incident was most significant to Holley, because it clearly proved to her both the Ouija board's reliability and her psychic sensitivity. One day she and a neighbor were using the board when a message seemed to break through. As Holley recalled it,

> "May is in trouble." We asked, "What is the trouble?" It answered, "With the sisters." Not knowing what prank she might have been

> guilty of for she was full of fun and mischief, I stopped writing with ouija, having the usual motherly feeling I suppose that I did not care to have my neighbor know about it, whatever it was.[1]

A day or so later a letter arrived from May asking that Marietta disregard her previous letter, which was never received, and saying that perhaps she had been to blame after all. Apparently the nuns had never mailed the first letter in which May complained about the nuns' reprimand and protested her innocence. Holley took the whole episode as proof that souls could communicate with each other by many means other than conventional ones. Holley had become addicted to the Ouija board, often using it daily, and she recorded many instances of communication, mostly concerning illness, death, or other loss. Sometimes the conclusions of the stories did not occur until months after a reading, when facts were confirmed, but most often the confirmation—or coincidence—was almost immediate, as in this case.

Most of Holley's friends were also involved in spiritualism and "Orientalism" or other forms of parapsychological play. The Carletons had a niece "who had the gift of automatic writing" and used it to engage them all during visits to the Thousand Islands.[2] In Washington, D.C., Clara Barton used a medium once or twice a week to contact the spirits of Theodore Parker, and Generals Sherman and Grant.[3] When Holley visited in New York City each spring, the coterie of friends would often visit a medium, although she always maintained that she had little faith in professional psychics. Mabel Wagnalls arranged one consultation for Holley after receiving a message that a friend who was ill in a nearby hotel had someone in the spirit world who wanted to see her. The spirit voice had stated her own name: Mary Holley. On the day of the seance, Mabel introduced Marietta as "Mrs. Allen," and the dramatic encounter commenced. There was the usual display of a cabinet and dim lights, and Holley described what happened as "much like an old-fashioned Methodist prayer meeting." The twenty or so paying guests sang old Methodist hymns until the first of the audience was called up to the cabinet to receive a spirit message. When Holley was summoned by a waif-spirit (in a white robe) named Bright-eyes, who said that Mary Holley wanted to speak with her, Holley's response was a mingling of fear and repulsion: "For my life I could not go. . . . When it came to the test, it seemed impossible for me to move from my seat . . . the thought of going any farther with my curiosity was repugnant to me."[4]

Rappings, manifestations, telepathy, spirit voices, and Ouija messages were all fascinating mysteries to Holley, even until death.

Like Samantha, she was moderate in her belief, although she spent much time in these later years dabbling in spiritualism, believing that Arthur Conan Doyle and Voltaire both communicated with her through the Ouija board. She even produced a short essay for the *World* magazine on the subject titled "What Is Behind Ouija?"[5] The piece is mostly anecdotal, showing how her faith in these matters wavered. Much of the material was later slipped into her autobiography, where she commented:

> I was always arguing in my mind whether what I saw and heard was from the psychic or the material world, from the quick or the dead. I suppose it was this state of mind that made it so hard for me to believe what it seemed so easy and natural for so many of my friends to place their confidence in.[6]

To her, whatever experiences she had were to remain in the realm of mystery, like religious faith. She shunned public displays, fostering her own sense that spiritualism was somehow an aspect of the divine intervention and guidance she believed in: "What proof I have had, and I am sure I have had proof of a power beyond my comprehension, has come in quiet hours nearly always when I was alone."[7]

Not all of Holley's time in New York City was spent with mediums and Ouija boards, of course. She continued to meet with her publishers to negotiate contracts. There were small dinner parties and literary receptions. It was at one of these latter that she said she met Mark Twain. In the 1870s Elisha Bliss had encouraged Holley to visit his home in Hartford, Connecticut, where she could meet Twain, Dudley Warner, H. B. Stowe, and others; but she had refused.[8] When True Williams, who illustrated both Twain's and Holley's works, told her that Twain was jealous of her, she declared that such talk was just "babble" probably caused by drink.[9] Twain had been kind though cryptic in his review of her second book. Very likely she felt some ambivalence about their being lumped into the same literary pile in New York City. She loved to tell how she first met Twain at a reception given for him. As she came next in line and her name was announced, he looked puzzled. It was obvious that he did not recognize her. In her soft, lisping voice she said, "Samantha," and he exclaimed heartily, "Samantha! I've always loved you."[10] In a curious reversal, she later denied in her autobiography that she had ever met Twain, although she had been invited to a banquet given in his honor. Both Lew and Ella remembered well Holley gleefully telling the story, and neither could account for the discrepancy.

A similar difficulty arises with another of her reminiscences. Supposedly the *New York World* concocted a publicity gimmick for Twain by asking famous authors to write his obituary while he was still very much alive. She demurred because it was late at night and she was tired, but the woman who made the request insisted, saying she would keep the telegraph office open a bit later if only Holley would comply. She dashed off a single sentence: "Death loves a shining Mark." The next Sunday's *World* showed Twain on the front page looking down at his tombstone under which appeared Holley's line.[11] Although she apoke of this with evident delight and pride, the whole episode remains unverified. Characteristically, she was very definite in her estimation of his works, feeling they were too sharply satiric. They lacked the "kindly wit and humor" of Burdette or Bret Harte or Booth Tarkington.

> I have nearly all of Twain's books I think in my library, but I am sorry to say that I don't believe I ever read one of them entirely through unless it was *Tom Sawyer*. I rather liked that, and also some of his magazine articles, especially the one he wrote after the untimely and tragic death of his daughter Jean. His heart spoke through that, and went to other hearts.[12]

Holley thrived on the life of the heart. She had loved a few persons deeply, and they were mostly absent from her during this period. Sylphina was nearly an invalid. Marietta hired not merely a maid, but a housekeeper-companion for them both, someone to stay behind to look after Finy and Bonnie View while Marietta continued her routine visits to Alexandria Bay and New York City. Clara was installed at Glen Echo, and they rarely met after 1900. However, when Clara was preparing to go to Russia in June 1902, Marietta lingered in New York City so that the two could spend the whole last day before her departure together.[13] Terrified as she was of deep water, Holley always feared that a journey across water would separate them in this life leaving her only the hope that they would be together in another one. Loss haunted her. In March 1903 Mrs. Flack died. When the estate was settled, her daughter wrote Marietta describing how the grand house she remembered had been converted into a home for crippled children, while the college buildings sat deserted and decaying.[14] Holley herself was frequently ill, but she continued to write. Most of the pieces were short magazine stories, but in September 1904 she did a two-part series on the Saint Louis Exposition for *Peterson's*. John H.

Cook, president of Dillingham Publishing Company, arrived at Bonnie View to buy book rights for the whole series, which was to be issued in November in both New York City and London, while the world's fair was still in progress.[15] When publication was announced, before the books were even issued, the publisher had received many orders for 1,000 copies from booksellers, and one order for 2,500 of the first edition.

Samantha at the St. Louis Exposition was the kind of book Holley had become known for. Samantha again plays the role of "observer and delineator," but she is worn out. The friendship between her and Josiah has deteriorated to "cold mockery."[16] When she stumbles in a description, she backs away from it with "I couldn't do justice to it, and so what is the use of tryin' with the Jonesville vocabulary."[17] Much of the material is old stuff, even to the phrasing. The issues are still temperance, morality, and suffrage; the incidents are vignettes taken from local life or copied from earlier works. Many characters are old ones with new names. Curiously, the work ends on a new note, as if Holley were weary with the formula. Samantha closes her narrative with fireworks—a metaphor of illumination, as she sees it—and the resolve to return home, but we do not see Samantha going back to the security of Jonesville.

There were many endings and beginnings for Holley in these first years of the new century. In July 1903 Marietta Holley Ford was married. The following June, after Miss Holley returned from New York City, May came home from the convent school bringing two friends with her.[18] On 30 June she married Fred Foley of Watertown. There is the strange absence of a wedding announcement in the Adams newspaper, especially when every visitor and movement at Bonnie View had been reported for several years. It may be that Holley disapproved of young Foley. In her book on children's rights six years later, Holley tells about a mother who wants to send her daughter to a convent for awhile to take her mind off marrying the wrong man. If this was not Holley's own concern, it may be simply that she felt May was too young to wed. Whatever her feelings, or the circumstances of the marriage, it seems that there was no lavish wedding. The couple moved to Glen Park, which was only a dozen miles north along the improved highway. Soon after, Marietta went to the Thousand Islands to rest and wrote from there to Clara at Glen Echo. Her friend's reply is revealing. She and George were having a farewell dinner together before Brother George left for California when "Samanthy's" letter arrived. The coincidence spurred a good deal of reminiscence, and the thought that they would "never all visit together again in *this* world."

Clara mentions that Pullman and his wife have adopted a little girl, much as Marietta had done, and closes the letter: "It is hard to realize that our little spright of a child can be eighteen and married. I realize that it has not been all happiness for you but how like a philosopher (as you are) you accept and carry it —"[19] Marietta's response to pain was, as always, to simply go on and have faith that things would work out.

Holley made trips within a limited circuit as these years passed. Finally in 1905 she bought an automobile, a Knox touring car specially made for her in Sringfield, Massachusetts. Lew was pressed into service again, this time to learn to drive. Years before, Elisha Bliss had known of Holley's fear of horses and sent her a photo of a horseless carriage in the streets of Hartford. Being as much afraid of the car as she was of the horses, she had delayed the purchase. By the time she had her own vehicle, the road in front of Bonnie View was often a hazard because of rambling motorists, and she was moved to comment when she got her first auto, "I do hope I will take more comfort than I did trying to flee from them."[20] She was financially comfortable, so the investment was no threat. Lew's salary had even been increased to thirty-five dollars a month. For that, he did her driving on the day trips around the region and some typing, although there were fewer manuscripts.

In March John Cook of Dillingham had called at Bonnie View again to arrange for the September publication of *Around the World with Josiah Allen's Wife* in book form.[21] Meanwhile she was putting together a book for Funk and Wagnalls, which she wanted to call *The Unseen Country*. It is really a pastiche of the stories of occult and psychic experiences that she had collected over the years from her friends. Most of the narratives appear in her autobiography, too. She had been noting them for years since her own interest was piqued, but in the text of the book she uses no names, only description enough so that anyone who knew her well would know that she was recounting events that supposedly happened to friends such as the Newmans, Wagnalls, Fords, Barton, and herself. Because the publisher would not allow the work to appear as it was, she added a weak strand to hang the stories on: Josiah has an accident with a borrowed auto, and while he is confined to bed, Samantha tries to entertain him by reading stories of "miraculous occurrences" out of a scrapbook she had kept. *Samantha Vs. Josiah* was a more saleable title, but the subtitle *Being the Story of the Borrowed Automobile and What Came of It* is both cumberson and misleading. Samantha insists, just as Holley did, that however incredible the tales might be, they were absolute fact. She has even included her own story about the minister's advice regarding the typewriter, although she does not identify herself as the writer in trouble. Also woven into the work is her own story of the divine intervention that she felt when she met Mother Prindle in New York City, a story that she expanded in her autobiography.[22] Holley had met Mother Prindle when the latter spoke at the Presbyterian Church in Mannsville of her mission to New York's down-and-out women. That was in September 1894,[23] and Holley dined afterward with the devout missionary. During supper Mother Prindle commented that the girls at the rescue mission enjoyed her books, and Holley offered to send copies for them. Soon afterward, Holley was in New York City and decided to visit the mission as soon as possible because the missionary was about to sail to Europe to open similar houses there. When Marietta was ready to leave the Murray Hill Hotel for the trip to the unsavory neighborhood where the home was, her companion was unable to go along. Holley issued a spur-of-the-moment invitation to a wealthy guest, Miss Kate Peck, who knew nothing of Prindle or the mission. In a spontaneous gesture of sisterhood, Miss Peck pledged to send Prindle money for a library and one hundred dollars for herself, which was precisely the amount that she lacked to be able to make her trip abroad. Holley believed that God's work was thus done through her.

> I felt that the Lord had honored me by using me as a messenger that day. . . . It seemed as if a road had been opened for me that day to walk in, by supernatural hands to carry the Lord's gift to His servant who was working for Him. Who could doubt that the Divine Presence was with us that day.[24]

Soon after *Samantha Vs. Josiah* appeared in 1906, May Shaver Foley gave birth to Francis Foley. The following February, May bore another child and named her Marietta Ruth. About this time, Holley took May's young brother Carl in, just as she had done with other stray boys, giving him a job on the estate.[25] After several weeks he fell ill, went to May's, and did not return.

Holley stayed very close to home all winter, hoarding her energies and protecting her precarious health. Her maid Rhoda, the one with "mediumistic powers," had left to be replaced by another black woman, Arabella Frank, but she did not stay long. By the next autumn she had abandoned the state of "single-blessedness" to marry a Watertown man.

In the autumn of 1907 May began to visit Marietta at Bonnie View, arriving with her two children for short visits. Whatever rift might have been caused by her marriage to Foley, the babies seemed to have healed it. May sometimes brought her young husband along, too. Then at Christmastime in 1907, May and the children spent a week with Holley before leaving to join her husband in Albany where he had been transferred.[26] Albany was much farther away than Glen Park, especially for a woman whose tolerance for travel was diminished. She had had a minor accident in her Knox: the car had skidded on the new road and had run through barbed wire fence.[27] Nevertheless, she bought a new team (guaranteed not to be afraid of automobiles) and a new sleigh in preparation for being out a good deal. In the spring of 1908 May, Fred, and the children returned to Bonnie View to visit her. When they left, she made her annual trip to New York City by train.

During the visit to New York City in June 1909, she contracted with Dillingham for her next book, which she had been working on for some time: *Samantha on Children's Rights*. Her experience raising May and her observation of May as a mother contributed to the quality of this work, although it still lacks the vigor of her earlier prose. She hoped to speak for the experience of all women: mothers, daughters, sisters, wives. Elizabeth Cady Stanton got wind of the project and sent her a letter with a copy of her own book *Eighty Years and More*. She commented on the importance of Holley's undertaking: "What I suffered in childhood from fear of parents, teachers, God and the Devil may give you some hints. Read my chapters on Babies and Divorce. . . . I show that the first right every baby has is to be well-borne."[28]

Holley believed in the redemptive possibilities of women, especially mothers. The rights in the title are more accurately the obligations of the parent and are grounded in her belief that parents are to children as God is to all. In the tradition of the nineteenth-century sentimental writers, Holley maintains that children are given to earthly parents only to "train up for higher service,"[29] and one may expect a child to be claimed, or called back, whenever God and the child are ready. Samantha advocates gentleness and moderation in everything but love. Children need attention, wholesome food, sensible clothing, a sound grounding in the Bible (just the inspiring, humane parts), biological mothers rather than foreign nursemaids, and healthy books to read rather than the cursed dime novels. *Children's Rights* was only mildly successful. Reviewers were tolerant, commenting that her eloquence had lost its freshness and that "popularity raises an author above criticism."[30]

Her public was faithful, but a new generation was buying new writers' works. The years had brought Holley veneration, even as her popularity dipped. Those same years had been healing ones for her relationships with her neighbors. In her seventies herself, she had outlived most of the folk who had criticized her out of envy and mistrust. Many of the younger people were proud to have a famous author living nearby, even if they did not read her books. Of those who did, some still insisted that she could not spell or write any better than she did in her books, and they marveled at the wealth such writing had won for her.

Like many North Country people, Holley believed that one's dress and habits should show off one's success, so she made a small display of her silk gowns and diamond jewelry. Even now, people in the area mention that no one ever saw her in an apron, thereby suggesting that she never had to wear one. In fair weather she would dress and summon her driver to take her out for an airing in either the carriage drawn by the cream-colored horses with tassels and bows on their braided manes and tails or in her equally elegant car.[31] Sometimes she would call for one of the local girls to accompany her to Adams for a treat at the ice cream parlor.[32] Often when she went out, she would take along a bouquet from her own gardens. The chauffeur would go to the door of the house Holley had chosen to visit and announce that Miss Holley would like to call if it was convenient.[33] Of course it usually was. Her eyes sparkling, her face alive with curiosity and kindness, she would exchange a short conversational volley, leave the flowers, and depart.

Her gardens still attracted many, old and young. Occasionally she would spot one of the local girls walking by and stop her to offer her a bunch of Bonnie View roses, then send the handyman to pick them. One small girl from up the road was spied picking flowers one day. The consequence of her crime was both frightful and charming: Miss Holley insisted that she join her for lunch the following Saturday. The child Juanita was seated in the dining room at a table set with Limoges china and damask linens. A servant brought in luncheon, then disappeared, unlike hired help who usually sat down with the family to eat. In fact, although Juanita did not notice, Holley breached etiquette by having her servant always serve her first at meals, a habit that caused considerable consternation among some of her guests.[34] Whether she did so out of ego or ignorance, it was a minor infraction more than compensated for by her kindness and generosity. As the girl looked anxiously at the finger bowls placed on the table, Miss Holley chuckled and told the child a funny story she recalled. She had been at a fancy dinner once, and a man who did not know any better drank out of one of the finger bowls instead of using it for its intended purpose.

Thereby, without embarrassing her, Marietta showed the child what the finger bowls were for.[35]

Such kindness did not cancel all the habits that irritated other neighbors. Holley ignored the truism that good fences make good neighbors. When the construction of the gardens and grounds was under way, Holley had torn up the old rail fences surrounding the property and pastures and replaced them with a low picket fence. Charming as it looked, it did not inhibit the cow's wandering. Daisy repeatedly got into the neighbors' corn. When they complained, Holley insisted that any other fence would spoil the look of the place. However, she wasn't insensitive to the complaints, so she agreed to put a string of barbed wire over the top of the pickets. Even that did not always work. One night, a neighbor who found the cow out simply took Daisy into the barn with his own cows and milked her. From that time on the cow was not allowed to roam freely.

Holley was a lenient overseer but proud of her Jersey cow, which gave more milk than the household could use. When butter was churned and turned into five-pound crocks, anything extra was sent to Cain's grocery in Adams to be bartered for credit, just as she had bartered her handiwork years before. Holley was pleased that there was a waiting list for people who wanted to buy "Bonnie View Butter."[36]

The near neighbors were usually tolerant of her ways, even when they seemed arrogant or more eccentric than usual. She still cherished her brood of prize hens. At dusk she would go into the yard and talk to them, mostly about the next day's weather, then call Ella and tell her what the forecast was.[37] The chickens were given as much freedom as the cow had been, until finally a neighbor tied a bit of string to a piece of corn and attached a note to the other end: "Keep your chickens home."[38]

Like Sarah Orne Jewett, Holley was sometimes unjustly accused of being condescending to the country folk, but the detractors merely misunderstood her manner. She simply did not know precisely how to create a relationship with those people, especially given her innate shyness. That is partly why she sought out children, creatures who would accept her small gifts without disdain or criticism.

By 1909 Holley's health was frail. In October she had a hand-operated elevator installed in the house so that she could more easily move between the floors. As that was being done, she received word of the death of her friend Mrs. Newman. As she wished, she had died in the Holy Land. Her ashes were being sent back for burial in her husband's grave near Saratoga Springs, but Marietta chose not to attend the burial ceremony.[39]

Lew Hoxie had left her employ four years earlier, returning only to type a manuscript when it was ready. She published less frequently in the periodicals, and most of the pieces were minor variations on the issue of woman's suffrage, such as the *Harper's Bazaar* piece called "Samantha Allen and the Auntys" in 1910. Holley truly believed that the vote was inevitable, if not imminent. Once in a while her works would be revived, many times for a charitable cause, particularly the play *Betsey Bobbet*. In February 1912 Holley created a new dramatic work, *Josiah's Secret*, to be performed at the opera house in Adams. The twenty-five-cent admission was intended to support the WCTU, and the piece was only the concluding segment of the evening's entertainment.[40] The play is barely sketched. There are only two characters, Samantha and Josiah. All three acts are set in the kitchen, the parlor, and the sitting room of the Allen home. There is no real drama, no movement on stage, and no change in their voices. The conflict is one Holley had included in several of the novels: Samantha is doing hard physical work, and Josiah explains about women not being strong enough to vote. Samantha had often before considered just sitting down and acting the part Josiah describes: being a "picture, allurin' and charmin'." Finally she does just that. He relents because he is starving and admits he is wrong (the "secret" of the title).[41] What is special about this play is that before this Samantha had only *considered* this technique of persuading Josiah, but by 1912 she is angry and impatient enough to do it.

Holley felt the press of time intensely. She had not had a letter from Clara Barton in nearly a year, and even that one was scribbled in secret against her doctor's orders. Barton ended with a declaration: "But I must tell you how it is with me, and that you are dearer to my heart than I could tell you with the strongest pen."[42] Clara's long silence and invalidism had prevented the women from sharing her last years, although they continued to love and pray for each other. That spring, at ninety, Clara died. A memorial service was held in Philadelphia, to which Holley was invited as a guest of honor. She considered attending, but with her fear of public appearances, her grief, and her own infirmities, she concluded, "I thought I could not go."[43] She did, however, write a loving tribute for a memorial book. Marietta was left to confront and reconcile her friend's death alone.

Holley was struggling to accommodate publishers' contracts and deadlines. Her works were almost entirely travel books and autobiography. With the success of *Around the World*, the editors at the *Christian Herald* tried to entice Holley to make a trip to the Holy Land for them. She refused. They then proposed a trip to Utah to investigate

Marietta Holley, circa 1910.

the "Mormon question." She again refused. She was busy with home and the writing that she could comfortably do in her own study rather than on a tour. They compromised, and she produced *Samantha at Coney Island and a Thousand Other Islands* in 1911. Most of the old characters appear, and Samantha recaptures some of her comic energy, but for the most part the book is a description of the sights Samantha enjoys. Now when she pauses to meditate, it is more often on the "Unknowable," faith, and spiritualism, rather than politics. The publishers wanted Holley to add a Coney Island section to the spare description of the Saint Lawrence River, and she tacked on an episode wherein Samantha chases Josiah to Coney Island. The latter resort makes an implicit—and unfavorable—contrast to the Thousand Islands. With typical regional pride Samantha declares that little of value is lost when fire sweeps the downstate resort. The actual fire at Coney Island had occurred while she was in New York City working on the manuscript; those details were merely incorporated into her book. She always regretted that the work had not been allowed to stand as she intended it, with just the Thousand Islands trip described,[44] but she was eager to continue publishing and was thus willing to compromise with a publisher.

In 1913 *Samantha on the Woman Question* was issued by the Fleming H. Revell Company, a publisher that was known for its religious books. For the first time in her career, Holley's name took precedence over her pseudonym on the title page. Believing that she was writing to a new wave of feminists, she did not hide behind the evasive titles of the earlier books. Perhaps she hoped that the new audience would not recognize the old material. Most of this book is recycled or recopied wholesale from *Sweet Cicely,* with a new framework added: Samantha goes to Washington, D.C., to see the women's rally and attend the Allen family reunion. Other than that, the narrative and dialogue remain intact; only names are changed. The seventy-seven-year-old writer was exhausted and crippled by her inability to compose her work by hand.

The next year she tried something that seemed very different, as though she had recovered some of her old energy. For Revell she produced *Josiah Allen on the Woman Question,* which is the only work written from Josiah's point of view. He begins by remarking that the only reason he did not write anything before was because he did not want to upset Samantha and ruin her cooking. Not surprisingly, the arguments are Josiah's, but the voice is Samantha's. As if her patience had run out, Samantha is letting Josiah run on in his absurdities, assuming that any right-minded person in the twentieth century would recognize his foolishness. It almost works, and at least Samantha has an opportunity to express her hope for the future of marriage after women get the vote when she envisions a utopia in Illinois where women had been enfranchised. The new book appeared just as the Coney Island book was reappearing. In spite of its literary flaws, the latter was popular. Originally it had been given as a premium to new subscribers by the *Christian Herald,* so it had been advertised only among its readers. Three years later it was published in twenty-five-cent and fifty-cent editions for the public. The first edition of 21,500 copies had sold out in a few months at the summer resorts, book stores, and depots where it was being marketed. A second, cheaper edition was out for the late summer.[45]

The year 1914 ended with the lukewarm reception of *Josiah Allen on the Woman Question.* One review kindly called the work "persuasive." It claimed that "in prose literature [Holley] stands with James Whitcomb Riley in poetry. They both belong to the common people."[46] However, industrialism, empire building, and urbanization had changed American humor. The rustic philosopher and small-town comic were replaced by immigrants who occupied the brimming cities. After the turn of the century, the old-style farmer was no longer the symbolic American. Horse-sense humor declined in popularity as more people were educated, and bad grammar, odd spelling, and colloquial speech seemed to demonstrate "inadequacy."[47] In her own time, Holley had felt the sting of this misreading: "There were . . . sympathetic ones who were sorry the writer could not spell better, and argued, hopefully, the she might even at this late day learn to spell more correctly if she applied herself to study.[48]

She recognized how anachronistic her work was. As she wrote her autobiography, she looked at a group of writers who wrote "unrestrained talk of most intimate things," authors who were cynical in the extreme, professing little belief in anything, especially anything "spiritual and divine."[49] To a friend who sent books to fill the quiet times she complained that she wearied of reading the newest works: "One gets tired of the ever-present triangle—husband, wife and villain—which appears now in almost every poem or short story."[50] Women's fiction had deteriorated until she could no longer sanction it as a vehicle for feminist ideas. Furthermore with the 1915 publication of Edgar Lee Masters' Spoon River Anthology, the small-town idealism was overshadowed by a more satiric realism. The sentimental pastoralism that Jonesville represented was out of fashion.[51] Samantha's time had passed.

The new year brought the death of May's husband at thirty-two. The body was brought back for burial in the rural cemetery.[52] Two months later, on 25 February, Sylphina died after being ill for several weeks. A private funeral was held at the house, and she was buried with the sisters' parents in Pierrepont Manor. There was no announcement of the death or funeral until a week later. She died, as she had lived, in seclusion. Ella became increasingly important to her aged Aunt Min. She was active in the WCTU and suffrage organizations, often serving as hostess for meetings. Holley was still the honorary president of the WCTU in Adams, but her function was almost entirely symbolic. As Holley withdrew into Bonnie View's quiet, Ella filled some of the aching loneliness for her. May had remained in Albany after her husband's death. When her father died in February 1916, she did not come back for the funeral. Will Shaver had arrived drunk in Adams on the train from Watertown. He was put into the lockup, but when it became clear that he was ill, a doctor was called. Before morning he died of "the complications of drink."[53] May's life was finally divorced from that of her father and brother. In May she married Arthur Patterson, a businessman from Glens Falls.

For the first time in many years Holley did not make a spring trip into New York City. She was negotiating with an unnamed movie company in Los Angeles that was to put some of the trials of Betsey, Samantha, and Josiah on film in an adaptation of the play *Betsey Bobbet*. It was her second venture into the world of film, but neither was successful, and she concluded that writing for the movies was "a sheer waste of time and energy."[54]

Holley turned from business to housekeeping. She and Matie Seamans did a thorough housecleaning. Marietta directed that many letters and old manuscripts be burned, saving only documents that bore the signatures of famous people. The old typewriter was given to Lew Hoxie. In the spring, May and her children visited Bonnie View, bringing her second husband to meet the aging mistress. She was nearing eighty, although no one guessed it from her bearing, when she was invited to join in the eightieth brithday celebration for William Dean Howells in New York City, which she could not attend.[55] On 20 May 1917, her elder sister Angeline died at ninety-three. Ella was all she had left of the circle of women who had loved her.

Death and war threatened Holley's peace. At the Giddingsville Bridge soldiers were guarding the railroad crossing. Holley contributed quilting blocks to the Garden Road Red Cross and bought one thousand dollars worth of Liberty Bonds.[56] The Civil War had been a distant emergency; this war was brought home to the neighborhood.

Although she was lonely, Holley was never actually alone. A

companion, usually Matie Seamans, was always at home with her. She still enjoyed her limousine rides on bright afternoons. The war's end focused her attention again on women's issues, but she could not write. In September 1919 May and the children arrived to stay for a week before they joined her husband in Jersey City.[57] Then Ella was gone, too. Her husband died suddenly of septic poisoning, and Ella went to Pennsylvania to live with her son.[58] The years passed in a litany of illnesses and recoveries. A few old friends visited, but most were dead. Ella traveled up from Williamsport when she could, but that was infrequently.

One new friend, Harold B. Johnson, the editor of the *Watertown Daily Times,* continued to visit and encourage her. He would drive down to call, sometimes taking with him his son John. More often they wrote letters, and Holley always inquired after the health of "little John," who was Johnson's only child. She even sent roses when he was ill with some childhood malady. In 1922 Johnson visited Marietta and asked her to write her autobiography. She protested that no one would be interested in her life, that nothing interesting had ever happened to her. Johnson persisted by sending her a pile of autobiographies: Henry Cabot Lodge's *Youthful Memories,* John Burroughs' *My Boyhood,* Hamlin Garland's *Son of the Middle Border,* and Brand Whitlock's *Forty years Of It.*[59]

Johnson probably never knew that as early as 1918 she had begun recording some of the circumstances of her life and writing, although it is unclear whether she intended ever to publish the autobiographical material. She read the autobiographies and returned them with a note insisting that she had no story of her own to tell.[60] In April she wrote him that she was "practically a shut-in," able to go up to her rooms only by the elevator. When she was invited by the French government to accompany twenty-seven other writers from the Author's League of America, she could not go.[61] Many of her works, having been translated into French, were popular there, but even the lure of international acclaim was not enough to revitalize her diminished energy. More and more she was looking inward and beyond.

In the summer of 1923 she placed a new monument on the Holley plot in the cemetery next to the Episcopal Church in Pierrepont Manor. It is a Celtic cross of granite that reaches nine feet at the top. On its circular center is blazoned IHS; across the base in raised letters is the name Holley. The monument displays a severe grandeur in its simplicity, standing in marked contrast to the weeping figures and lachrymose poetry of markers that were typical during this period as well as to the plain stones that fill the rest of the churchyard.[62]

During the winter of 1923 she worked on her autobiography as if she were struggling to tie up the strands of her life. She wrote Johnson about the manuscript.

> It lies neglected. I would love to have you read 20 or 30 pages of the beginning to see what you thought of it—I never felt so about any of my other books, never thought of showing them to anyone—
>
> I am very sure I could get a publisher to undertake it but I don't know that I want it published—when I was hiding my own personality behind Samantha—I could say what I chose—but now it is like coming out of the welcome twilight into the hot blaze of noon.
>
> I was always too reticent and backward about speaking of things that interested me the most deeply, and therefore it is hard to decide whether I want it published or not.[63]

Later she wrote him this reminder: "A hen doesn't cackle until its egg is laid."[64] In the spring she again did some housecleaning, listing the piles of letters that the housekeeper was directed to take out of the attic. With that completed, she summoned Johnson to Bonnie View. When he appeared in her study she said she had something to show him. "I feel like a hen who has stolen her nest."[65] She opened the drawer and produced a manuscript of several hundred pages. After Johnson had looked at it he asked why she had included little or nothing about her family. She quickly added chapter 27 to satisfy him. She called the work "About My Books and Interesting People I Have Met." Johnson agreed that she would retain the manuscript until her death. In the introduction (which he did not print) she demurred, "This book in no sense pretends to be a formal autobiography, with dates and statistics, for I have not had enough striking events in my life to make such a volume interesting."[66] In the tradition of the feminine biographies of the middle decades of the nineteenth century, there are no dates. She extends the convention further though, because the whole work does not even bear the "organic markers—birth, conversion, marriage, death"—of the earlier women's biographies.[67] As if to hide herself and deny her age, there is no chronology; events are linked by ideas or characters rather than time. She told Johnson: "I have been careful not to speak too much of myself. Josiah was never an egotistical man. Samantha took all the egotism out of him and if I was ever egotistical life has taken it out of me."[68] Holley made curious corrections in her manuscript copy: compound sentences are changed to complex sentences; minor shifts are made in word choice ("decided suffragette" to "ardent suffragette," "shirt" to "clothes"); and sentences are rewritten to shift focus away from herself ("When I visited Miss Wiggins" to "When Miss Wiggins visited, I was with her"). Most particularly she crossed out names, or parts of names, so that actors in the narrative are identified only as "a neighbor" or "Mrs. W."

In spite of the pecularities, Holley felt that it was finished, and she set about enjoying her summer days. Ella visited and stayed nearly three weeks for a good old-fashioned visit.[69] Sitting in her room overlooking the gardens, Marietta asked Ella if she would like to have Bonnie View because she hated to see it go to someone outside of the family. Ella replied that she would never want to live there without her. Marietta, sensing that it might be their final visit, commented that it was sad to be the last of one's family. She added, "Sometimes I feel I made a great mistake in not marrying" and read aloud several old love letters. She had refused all offers, saying Josiah needed her.[70] After Ella left in July, Holley bought another new car, her fourth. In October she made her final will. Lew Hoxie paid her a visit, and she told him, as if saying farewell, "We are placed here, we don't know why, and we go away, we don't know where." At Christmas she was still the usual witty, self-possessed woman her family expected to see. None realized that she was eighty-nine years old. In the final chapter of her autobiography, she had written that she had lived to her old age in "a triumph of mind over matter." With the same will, she approached her death.

In early January Holley was ill, but no one suspected she was near death because she had often been so much sicker and had still recovered. The family complained of her physician Dr. Minar, protesting that he was not moral. She replied, "I want skill when I'm sick, not morality."[71] She probably knew that what the family believed to be a passing stomach ailment was cancer. She had confided to Johnson that she thought she wanted to die in spring because it was a more friendly time.[72] In the deep winter of 1874, fifty-two years earlier, she had penned "A Dream of Spring" that ended:

> The world is asleep—all hushed
> is nature's warm, sweet breath;
> The world is asleep, and dreaming
> the silent dream of snow;
> But through the silence that seems
> like the silence of death,
> Under the shroud of ermine the
> souls of the roses glow.

On the last day of February 1926, she wrote out the verse that Mark Twain had had carved on his daughter Susan's tombstone:

Warm summer sun, shine brightly here,
Warm southern winds, blow softly here,
Green sods above, lie light, lie light,
Good night, dear heart, good night, good night.

She laid the paper on her bedside table and drifted into sleep.[73]

That night Ella was asleep in Pennsylvania, unaware of Marietta's condition, when she had a strange dream or vision: she was emerging from some sort of entertainment when a friend stopped her to say, "Ella, Aunt Min wants to see you." She saw Marietta plainly in the distance, smiling, then fading away.[74]

The next day, 1 March, it was clear that Marietta was indeed fading although she remained conscious. A wild March storm had begun. Wind-driven snow made it nearly impossible to get anyone to the house. Only her nephew Will, Matie Seamans, a neighbor woman, and the doctor were with her. The window shades were drawn. There was no one to savor the view. Ironically none of those present thought to record her last words. She had created many poignant deathbed scenes but left no one to recreate hers. When she died at two o'clock that afternoon, a tiny circle of kin, neighbors, and friends ringed the bed, and there was no Josiah among them.[75]

EPILOGUE

THE STORM CONTINUED through the following day. Snow blocked the roads and delayed trains. May could not return to Bonnie View for the funeral. She was living in Saint Louis with her third husband, Leslie Barksdale, and she and one of the children were ill. When the honorary pallbearers could not break through the storm to attend the quiet service at the house, four neighbors loaded the body onto the sleigh for the trip to Adams, where it was kept in the cemetery vault until spring.[1]

In early May a memorial service was held at the Adams Baptist Church. The church was filled with members from all the congregations in town. The diversity testified to Holley's Christian rather than sectarian appeal. The poem that Whittier had pronounced perfect, "The Deacon's Daughter," was read, and a collection taken up to further the generous works that Holley had initiated.[2] After the public memorial, a cluster of family went quietly to the churchyard at Pierrepont Manor. Mr. Hancock, Marietta's friend from the Hope Sabbath School, officiated at the interment. Her own headstone had been placed when the Holley monument was set, but she had left off a birthdate. After searching the records, the family was astonished to find that her age had been only three months shy of ninety. Her dates were chiseled on the plain low marker that matched those of her father, mother, and sister. At the graveside stood Ella Copeland and Will Page, Holley's niece and nephew. May, her husband, and Francis joined them. Neither of Holley's other namesakes were present.[3]

Within ten days an auction was held to dispose of the remnants of Holley's household things that she had not willed away. Her brass bed sold for twenty-seven dollars; the melodeon brought twelve; her sleigh went for three-and-a-half dollars; the narrow, slant-topped desk on which she wrote most of her books was bought for only seventy-five cents.[4]

Her total estate amounted to nearly $100,000.[5] Much of that was given to charities. The Adams Baptist Church, the public libraries in Adams and Pierrepont Manor, the Pierrepont Manor Cemetery Association, and the Jefferson County Orphans Home received substantial gifts. Holley had instructed Matie Seamans to burn all her unpublished manuscripts and all other papers except for some letters bearing the signatures of celebrities. A copy of the autobiography seems to have been snatched from the fire.[6] Another copy, corrected, went to Johnson, who began publishing it in 1931. The few letters were given to the Jefferson County Historical Society.

Seventeen years later a woman claimed to have discovered old letters proving that Marietta had been romantically involved with Will Seymour Monroe, a man twenty-five years her junior. The interpretation of the letters—if indeed they exist—is absurd. Monroe had kept up a correspondence with Twain and Whitman, and was himself a much-published nonfiction writer. It is possible that Twain suggested Monroe approach Holley for an interview or advice, and they might have exchanged letters, but anything more is at best unlikely.[7] Holley had been careful to eclipse the names of her suitors and destroy letters that were very private to ensure that only her public self would remain. Her portrait by Pine was given to the Flower Memorial Library in Watertown, where it still hangs in a vaulted marble room off the main lobby.

Each of her remaining family was remembered in her will, as were the employees who had served her faithfully. Besides money, she left gifts that showed a loving interest in their daily lives. To Will Page she gave her auto. Ella was given the Victrola and records. Marylyn Page received part of her personal library and the much-used pianola. May's children received one thousand dollars each. May herself—named in the will as Marietta Holley Barksdale—was bequeathed three thousand dollars and Marietta's diamond solitaire ring. Lew Hoxie received a portion of her library and her Bible. There was no provision made for the parrot, the only pet that remained. Lew, even though he was embittered at being slighted in the will, bought the forty-year-old bird from the executors.[8] Everything else was left to Ella, May, and a niece named Theresa Page—everything but Bonnie View itself.

The house, barns, and seven acres were left to the Salvation

Army along with four thousand dollars for maintenance. The place was to be "used as an eventide home for aged and friendless women."[9] For three years the army used it as a home for invalids and children of army families, but in 1930 that function was abandoned and the place was left in a caretaker's charge. He rented it to tourists, so the land became taxable. The tax levied went unpaid until Bonnie View was sold at the tax auction in August 1938 for $55.59. The purchaser gave the property title back to the Salvation Army. It took that organization another nine years to modify the buildings and grounds to accommodate those for whom Holley had intended it. In July 1947 Harold B. Johnson dedicated Bonnie View to its mission. Lew and the parrot were both dead by then, but some of Polly's bright green feathers were displayed under glass on the wall of the front hall. It was the sort of gesture that would have either delighted or horrified Holley herself. Nevertheless, Bonnie View was being used in a way that she would have approved: as a summer residence and rest home for underprivileged mothers and children brought from the cities to enjoy the lovely North Country summers.[10]

In his dedicatory address and his journal, Johnson noted that Bonnie View was alive with the phantoms of Holley's characters and her own strong spirit. On the back of the program for the day's ceremony was quoted the last poem she is known to have written, probably in the summer of 1925.

Bonnie View

The sunrise softer, sweeter glows,
The sunset has a brighter rose,
The summer's golden glories seem
To gild the earth with warmer gleam—
And deeper seems the skies far blue
Above the fields of Bonnie View.

And in the future from afar
Perhaps from unfamiliar star
Shall I permitted be to gaze
Upon these dear familiar ways?
Or walk unseen the gardens thru
The flowery paths of Bonnie View.

Or will the "place" awaiting me
So full of blest fulfillment be?
Will weary hearts homesick and tossed
Find recompense for all they lost?
Shall I, dear heart, content with you,
Forget my old home Bonnie View?

Today few remember Marietta Holley. The New York State historical marker in front of her house (which is again a private residence) mentions Samantha. The birthdate given on the marker is incorrect. Garden Road is a three-lane highway that took over a third of the gardens that Holley had created from the cedar swamp. Where fish splashed and little girls rambled over arched bridges, a tangled thicket chokes out all but a few wildflowers.

NOTES

PROLOGUE

1. Linda Ann Finton Morris, "Women Vernacular Humorists in Nineteenth Century America: Ann Stephens, Frances Whitcher, and Marietta Holley," Ph.D. diss. University of California, Berkeley, 1978, pp. 2, 50–53.

2. Thomas F. O'Donnell, "The Regional Fiction of Upstate New York," Ph.D. diss. Syracuse University, 1957, p. 41.

3. Marietta Holley, *My Opinions and Betsey Bobbet's* (Hartford, Ct.: American Publishing, 1873), p. 247.

4. Marietta Holley, *Josiah Allen's Wife as P.A. and P.I.: Samantha at the Centennial* (Hartford, Ct.: American Publishing, 1877), pp. 399–400.

5. Marietta Holley, *Samantha at The St. Louis Exposition* (New York: Dillingham, 1904), pp. 157–59.

6. Eleanor Flexner, *Century of Struggle: The Woman's Rights Movement in the United States*, rev. ed. (Cambridge, Ma.: Harvard University Press, 1975), pp. 185–88.

7. Nina Baym, *Woman's Fiction: A Guide to Novels by and about Women in America, 1820–1870* (Ithaca: Cornell University Press, 1978), pp. 11–12.

8. Gail Parker, ed., *The Oven Birds: American Women on Womanhood 1820–1920* (New York: Anchor Books, 1972), p. 4.

9. Ann Douglas Wood, "The Literature of Impoverishment: The Women Local Colorists in America, 1865–1914," *Women's Studies* 1 (1972): 3–45.

1—WOODLAND AND FARM

1. Katherine Gillette Blyley, "Marietta Holley," Ph.D. diss. University of Pittsburgh, 1936, p. 2. Blyley's work has been the most thorough and reliable source of bio-

graphical material. Begun within the decade of Holley's death, the research included interviews with acquaintances of Holley's who have since died. As a record of impressions and elusive facts, Blyley's work is invaluable. However, since her work, documents and papers that both support and refute her views have become available, which answer and raise more questions about Holley's life.

2. Marietta Holley, "The Story of My Life," published serially in the *Watertown Daily Times*, Watertown, N.Y., 5 February to 9 April 1931. Because the work is divided into chapters that are sometimes spread over different days' editions, all citations are given with chapter number rather than date.

3. S. W. Durant and H. B. Pierce, *History of Jefferson County, New York* (Philadelphia: Everts, 1878), pp. 242–43.

4. Ibid., pp. 22–23; 244.

5. Holley, "Story," chapter 26.

6. Durant and Pierce, *History of Jefferson County*, p. 244.

7. The Taber name is also found spelled Tabor; I have used Holley's preferred spelling.

8. *National Cyclopedia of American Biography, s.v.* "Marietta Holley"; Blyley, "Marietta Holley," p. 3 n.

9. Whitney R. Cross, *The Burned-Over District: The Social and Intellectual History of Enthusiastic Religion in Western New York, 1800–1850* (New York: Harper and Row, 1955). pp. 4–5.

10. Holley, "Story," chapter 27.

11. Durant and Pierce, *History of Jefferson County*, p. 560.

12. Ibid., pp. 547–48. Rosemary Nesbitt continues the tradition of North Country pride in this event in her fictionalized account for young readers, *The Great Rope* (Oswego, N.Y.: Mathom, 1980).

13. *New York State Census*, 1835.

14. Ella Page Copeland, "Memories of Marietta Holley By One Who Knew Her Well," *Watertown Daily Times*, 10 October 1936. Ms. Copeland was Holley's niece, the daughter of her sister Angeline Page.

15. Durant and Pierce, *History of Jefferson County*, p. 255.

16. Barbara Welter, *Dimity Convictions* (Athens, Oh.: Ohio University Press, 1976), p. 86.

17. Ella Page Copeland, "Home Memories of Marietta Holley and Her Family," *Watertown Daily Times*, 23 November 1934.

18. Holley, "Story," chapter 27.

19. Mary Celeste Williamson, "Marietta Holley's Samantha," M.A. thesis, Catholic University of America, 1946, p. 14.

20. Ibid.

21. Copeland, "Home Memories."

22. Holley, "Story," chapter 1. Because Holley wrote primarily dialect prose with its odd usages and orthography, much of the material quoted here is nonstandard. The use of *sic*, although it is technically correct, is cumbersome and disruptive in this case. Therefore, I have omitted it hereafter when quoting from Holley's works and letters.

23. Ibid.

24. Thomas F. O'Donnell, in his dissertation, "The Regional Fiction of Upstate New York," Syracuse University, 1957, p. 235, n. 17, notes that a John Milton Holley, Jr., attended Hamilton College in Hamilton, N.Y., in 1866 and suggests that Marietta's sense of being slighted in her schooling may have contributed to her feminist sentiments. However, if the John Holley at Hamilton was in fact her brother, he would have attended at the age of thirty-four, which is an unlikely prospect. There is much reliable evidence that her brother John went west with his brothers and stayed there.

25. Durant and Pierce, *History of Jefferson County*, pp. 240–42.

26. Hamilton Child, ed., *Gazetteer and Business Directory of Jefferson County, New York, 1866–67* (Watertown, N.Y: New York Reformer, 1866), p. 18.

27. Durant and Pierce, *History of Jefferson County*, pp. 253–54; 257. This hall is the same one referred to in chapter 3 as the Cooper Opera House.

28. Holley, "Story," chapter 1.

29. Cross, *Burned-Over District*, p. 3.

30. Ibid., p. 349.

31. Holley, "Story," chapter 1.

32. Ibid., chapter 2.

33. R. Lawrence Moore, "Spiritualist Mediums: A Study of Female Professionals in Victorian America," *American Quarterly* no. 29 (1972): 478.

34. Harold B. Johnson, dedicatory speech at Holley's home, Pierrepont Manor, N.Y., 13 July 1947, p. 4, in the possession of John B. Johnson.

35. Holley, "Story," chapter 1.

36. Copeland, "Memories."

37. Blyley, "Marietta Holley," p. 4.

38. This scrapbook is in the possession of Henry and Anita Colby, Pierrepont Manor, N.Y.

39. Blyley, "Marietta Holley," p. 4.

40. "Two of Marietta Holley's Manuscripts Found," *Watertown Daily Times*, Watertown, N.Y., 13 March 1945.

41. Holley, "Story," chapter 3.

42. Durant and Pierce, *History of Jefferson County*, p. 110, and Cross, *Burned-Over District*, pp. 17–18.

43. Holley, "Story," chapter 1.

44. Cross, *Burned-Over District*, p. 323.

45. Durant and Pierce, *History of Jefferson County*, p. 109.

46. Cross, *Burned-Over District*, p. 173.

47. Ibid., p. 177.

48. Nancy F. Cott, *The Bonds of Womanhood: "Woman's Sphere" in New England, 1780–1835* (New Haven: Yale University Press, 1977), p. 159.

49. Durant and Pierce, *History of Jefferson County*, p. 109.

50. Barton M. Enos, "Conversion of Josiah Allen's Wife," *Watertown Daily Times*, no date.

51. Holley, "Story," chapter 27.

52. Ella Page Copeland, "More Memories of Marietta Holley and Her Family," *Watertown Daily Times,* 28 December 1934.

53. Copeland, "Home Memories."

54. Holley, "Story," chapter 3.

55. Cott, *Bonds of Womanhood,* p. 115

56. Blyley, "Marietta Holley," p. 5.

57. Carl Bode, *Anatomy of American Popular Culture* (Berkeley: University of California Press, 1959), p. 21.

58. Holley, "Story," chapter 3.

59. Jerome B. Holley to Marietta Holley, undated cited in *Watertown Daily Times,* Watertown, N.Y., 15 February 1938.

60. Marietta Holley, "How I Wrote My First Book," *Harper's Bazar* 45, no. 9: September 1911, 404.

61. Holley, "Story," chapter 1.

62. Ibid.

63. Copeland, "Memories of Marietta Holley."

2—HEARTH AND GARDEN

1. *Jefferson County Journal,* 30 July 1857.

2. See Cott, *Bonds of Womanhood,* chapter 2.

3. Constance Rourke, *American Humor: A Study of the National Character* (New York: Harcourt, Brace, 1931). See particularly the section on Jack Downing, pp. 23–26.

4. Marietta Holley, "How I Wrote," p. 405.

5. Holley, "Story," chapter 2.

6. Mabel Wagnalls, "A Glimpse of Marietta Holley," *Ladies Home Journal* (Nov. 1903): 61.

7. Rourke, *American Humor,* p. 195.

8. Copeland, "Home Memories."

9. *Jefferson County Journal,* 12 June 1862.

10. Holley, "Story," chapter 3; and Copeland, "More Memories."

11. Holley, "Story," chapter 3.

12. Ibid.

13. Ibid.

14. Copeland, "More Memories."

15. Holley, "Story," chapter 13.

16. *Jefferson County Journal,* 31 October 1861.

17. Johnson, dedicatory speech, p. 3.

18. Durant and Pierce, *History of Jefferson County,* pp. 261–63.

19. *Jefferson County Journal,* 16 August 1859.

20. Ibid., 26 June 1860.

21. Holley, "Story," chapter 5; and *Jefferson County Journal,* 5 November 1879.

22. *Jefferson County Journal,* 8 September 1859.

23. Ibid., 27 April 1871.

24. Ibid., 1 June 1871.

25. Holley to Henry Wadsworth Longfellow, 10 March (no year), Houghton Library, Harvard University.

26. Holley, "Story," chapter 2.

27. Ibid., chapter 3.

28. Ibid., chapter 2.

29. Blyley, "Marietta Holley," p. 7.

30. "Fourth of July at Jonesville," *Peterson's* Magazine 56, no. 1 (July 1869): 54–57.

31. Holley, "How I Wrote," p. 404.

32. Ibid.

33. Holley, "Story," chapter 5.

34. Ibid., chapter 3.

35. Copeland, "Memories of Marietta Holley."

36. Holley, "Story," chapter 3.

37. DeLancey Ferguson, *Mark Twain: Man and Legend* (New York: Bobbs-Merrill, 1943), pp. 130–38.

38. Frank Luther Mott, *Golden Multitudes: The Story of Best Sellers in the United States* (New York: Macmillan, 1947), p. 155.

39. James D. Hart, *The Popular Book* (New York: Oxford University Press, 1950), p. 151.

40. Mott, *Golden Multitudes,* p. 156.

41. Rourke, *American Humor,* pp. 16 ff.

42. Jennette Tandy, *Crackerbox Philosophers in American Humor and Satire* (Port Washington, N.Y.: Kennikat Press, 1925), p. 47.

43. Marietta Holley, *My Opinions and Betsey Bobbet's.*

44. Rourke, *American Humor,* pp. 23–26

45. Tandy, *Crackerbox Philosophers,* p. 146.

46. Rourke, *American Humor,* p. 222.

47. Linda Ann Finton Morris, "Women Vernacular Humorists in Nineteenth Century America: Ann Stephens, Frances Whitcher, and Marietta Holley," Ph.D. diss. University of California, Berkeley, 1978, p. 50. Morris' chapters 4 and 5 provide an insightful analysis of Holley's style and place her in the humorous tradition.

48. Rourke, *American Humor,* p. 142.

49. Jane Curry, "Women as Subjects and Writers of Nineteenth Century American Humor," Ph.D. diss. University of Michigan, 1975, p. 27.

50. Walter Blair, *Native American Humor, 1800–1900* (New York: American Book, 1937), p. 49.

51. Hart, *Popular Book,* p. 142.

52. Morris, *Women Vernacular Humorists*, p. 160.

53. Blair, *Native American Humor*, pp. 121–23.

54. Rourke, *American Humor*, p. 212.

55. Rourke, *American Humor*, p. 227, Tandy, *Crackerbox Philosophers*, p. 158, and Wood, "Literature of Impoverishment," p. 13.

56. Wood, "Literature of Impoverishment," pp. 17–31.

57. Holley, "Story," chapter 4.

58. Holley, "How I Wrote My First Book," p. 404.

59. Copeland, "Memories of Marietta Holley"; and Holley, "Story," chapter 3.

3—HER PLACE IN TIME

1. Holley, "Story," chapter 4.

2. Only one of Holley's publishers, Funk and Wagnalls, has records about her publications, and those concern only the American market. According to Frank Luther Mott's criteria for a best-seller, a book must have had a total sale equal to one percent of the population of the United States for the decade in which it was published. This is misleading when works are republished over several decades, as some of Holley's were. The issue of popularity becomes a question of numbers and unreliable accountings.

3. Frank Luther Mott, *History of American Magazines, 1865–85* (Cambridge, Ma.: Harvard University Press, 1938), p. 224.

4. *Watertown Daily Times*, 29 March 1927.

5. Perry Westbrook, *Acres of Flint: Sarah Orne Jewett and Her Contemporaries*, rev. ed. (Metuchen, N.J.: Scarecrow Press, 1981), p. 100.

6. Nina Baym, *Woman's Fiction*, p. 188. Jonesville is a community much like Adams, N.Y. Loontown seems to be patterned after Watertown, the county seat. Other place names appear to indicate the location of these two fictional towns: Zoar, Lyme, Harrisville, Log London, etcetera.

7. Holley, *My Opinions and Betsey Bobbet's*, pp. 24–25.

8. Ibid., p. v.

9. Walter Blair, *Horse Sense in American Humor* (Chicago: Chicago University Press, 1942), p. 193.

10. Holley, *My Opinions and Betsey Bobbet's*, pp. 2–3.

11. Ibid., p. 4.

12. Ibid., p. 18.

13. Welter, *Dimity Convictions*, p. 77.

14. Holley, *My Opinions and Betsey Bobbet's*, p. 18.

15. Ann Douglas, *The Feminization of American Culture* (New York: Knopf, 1977), p. 71.

16. Gail Parker, "Introduction," *The Oven Birds: American Women on Womanhood, 1820–1920* (New York: Anchor Books, 1972), p. 15.

17. Curry, "Women As Subjects," p. 134.

18. Holley, *My Opinons and Betsey Bobbet's*, p. 26.

19. Wood, "Literature of Impoverishment," p. 10.

20. Holley, *The Widder Doodle's Love Affair and Other Stories* (New York: F. M. Lupton, 1893), p. 29.

21. Johnson, dedicatory speech, p. 10.

22. Douglas, *Feminization*, chapters 3 and 4.

23. Welter, *Dimity Convictions*, p. 86.

24. Holley, *My Opinions and Betsey Bobbet's*, p. 315.

25. *Jefferson County Journal*, 7 December 1871.

26. Ibid., 14 November 1872.

27. Barbara Ehrenreich and Deirdre English, *Complaints and Disorders: The Sexual Politics of Sickness* (Old Westbury, N.Y.: The Feminist Press, 1973), pp. 11–29.

28. Copeland, "Memories of Marietta Holley."

29. Juanita Shutts Jones, interview with author, 17 October 1981.

30. Helen Waite Papashvily, *All the Happy Endings* (New York: Harpers, 1956), p. 23.

31. Blyley, "Marietta Holley," p. 13.

32. *Jefferson County Journal*, 17 February 1875.

33. Holley, "How I Wrote My First Book," p. 404.

34. *Jefferson County Journal*, 24 May 1876.

35. Ibid., 15 November 1876.

36. Ibid., 5 November 1877.

37. *Woman's Journal*, Boston, 22 June 1878.

38. Holley, "Story," chapter 24.

39. Marietta Holley, *Samantha among the Brethren* (New York: Funk and Wagnalls, 1890), p. 204.

40. Foster Cooles, "A Visit to Josiah Allen's Wife," *New York Mail and Express*, 27 February 1892.

41. *Jefferson County Journal*, 30 January 1878.

42. Holley, "Story," chapter 20.

43. *Jefferson County Journal*, 29 September 1880.

44. Susan B. Anthony to Holley, 26 June 1878, in Flower Memorial Library, Watertown, N.Y.

45. Holley, "Story," chapter 5.

46. The originals of these cards are in the Jefferson County Museum, Watertown, N.Y.

47. *Jefferson County Journal*, 18 December 1873.

48. Diary of Clara Barton, July 1880, Manuscript Division, Library of Congress, Washington, D.C.

49. *Jefferson County Journal*, 31 March 1880.

50. Ibid., 5 May 1880 and 6 October 1880.

51. Marietta Holley, *The Lament of the Mormon Wife* (Hartford, Ct.: American Publishing, 1877), pp. 6, 8.

52. Jefferson County Journal, 21 July 1870.

53. Ibid., 23 February 1881.

54. Mrs. Russell Judson, "First Area College Left Mark on Village," *Chatham Courier Supplement,* 19 October 1972.

55. Holley, "Story," chapter 7.

4—THE GREAT TOUR

1. Holley, "Story," chapter 7, and *Jefferson County Journal,* 10 August 1881.

2. Holley, "Story," chapter 8.

3. Ibid., chapter 7.

4. Ibid., chapter 13.

5. Ibid., chapter 21.

6. Holley to True Williams, undated, Jefferson County Historical Society, Watertown, N.Y.

7. *Jefferson County Journal,* 24 August 1891.

8. Holley to True Williams, undated, Jefferson County Historical Society, Watertown, N.Y.

9. Holley, "Story," chapter 8.

10. Ibid., chapter 4.

11. *Jefferson County Journal,* 17 May 1882.

12. Holley, "Story," chapter 4.

13. *Jefferson County Journal,* 4 April 1883.

14. Holley, "Story," chapter 4.

15. *Jefferson County Journal,* 18 January and 9 August 1882.

16. Ibid., 5 July and 13 September 1882.

17. Marietta Holley, *Miss Richard's Boy and Other Stories* (Hartford, Ct.: American Publishing, 1883), p. viii.

18. Holley, "Story," chapter 4.

19. Ibid.

20. Baym, *Woman's Fiction,* chapters 1 and 2.

21. Holley, "Story," chapter 8.

22. Blyley, "Marietta Holley," p. 16.

23. *Jefferson County Journal,* 17 January 1883.

24. Holley, "Story," chapter 6.

25. Ibid., chapter 5, and *Jefferson County Journal,* 30 May 1883.

26. Holley, "Story," chapter 9.

27. *Jefferson County Journal*, 22 August 1883.

28. Ibid., 5 December 1883.

29. Blyley, "Marietta Holley," p. 29; see *Sweet Cicely: Josiah Allen as a Politician* (New York: Funk and Wagnalls, 1885), pp. 278 ff. for example.

30. R. Lawrence Moore, "Spiritualism and Science: Reflections on the First Decade of the Spirit Rappings," *American Quarterly*, 29 (1972): 477, 486.

31. *Jefferson County Journal*, 14 May 1884.

32. Susan B. Anthony to Holley, 29 May 1884, Flower Memorial Library, Watertown, N.Y.; and Holley, *Sweet Cicely*, pp. 160–1.

33. Cyrus H. K. Curtis to Holley, 20 September 1884, Flower Memorial Library.

34. Letters to Holley from McClure, 20 October and 25 October 1884, Flower Memorial Library.

35. S. S. McClure to Holley, 15 December 1884, Flower Memorial Library.

36. Holley, Story," chapter 6.

37. Mott, *History of American Magazines* IV: 39.

38. *Jefferson County Journal*, 10 March 1884.

39. Will Carleton to Holley, 3 March 1885, Flower Memorial Library.

40. *Jefferson County Journal*, 7 July, 15 December, and 17 November 1885.

41. Susan B. Anthony to Holley, 31 January 1886, Flower Memorial Library.

42. Holley to Rose Cleveland, 1885 (no other date), Minnesota Historical Society; and Cleveland to Holley, 11 February 1886, Flower Memorial Library.

43. Baym, *Woman's Fiction*, p. 267.

44. Herbert Ross Brown, *The Sentimental Novel in America* (Durham, N.C.: Duke University Press, 1942), p. 201.

45. Aileen S. Kraditor, *The Ideas of the Woman Suffrage Movement, 1890–1920* (New York: Columbia University Press, 1965), pp. 66–67.

46. Holley, *Sweet Cicely*, p. 109.

47. Ibid.

48. *Jefferson County Journal*, "About Sweet Cicely," 2 March 1886.

49. Ibid., 4 May and 8 June 1886.

50. Holley, "Story," chapter 14.

51. *Jefferson County Journal*, 22 June, 6 July, and 27 July 1886.

52. Holley, "Story," chapters 10 and 11.

53. Ibid., chapter 11, and C. K. Curtis to Holley, 17 May 1888, Jefferson County Historical Society, Watertown, N.Y.

54. Holley, "Story," chapter 14.

55. Ibid., chapter 20.

56. *Jefferson County Journal*, 12 April 1887.

57. Holley, "Story," chapter 18.

58. Clara Barton's biographers disagree about when and where Holley and Barton first met. By comparing their itineraries and Holley's own account of how and where they met, I conclude that the meeting must have taken place during this trip to Washington, D.C.

59. Blanche Colton Williams, *Clara Barton: Daughter of Destiny* (New York: Lippincott, 1941), pp. 39–40.

60. Ibid., pp. 42, 129, 142.

61. Ibid., p. 133.

62. Ibid., pp. 214, 263.

63. Holley, "Story," chapter 19.

64. Papashvily, *Happy Endings,* p. 74.

65. Holley, "Story," chapter 5.

66. Ibid., chapter 19.

67. Ibid.

68. *Jefferson County Journal,* 19 July, 9 August, and 30 August 1887.

69. Will Carleton to Holley, 24 July 1887, Flower Memorial Library.

70. Ibid., 9 September 1887, Flower Memorial Library.

71. Irving Bacheller to Holley, 25 March 1887; S. W. Foss to Holley, 16 January 1888, Flower Memorial Library.

72. Marietta Holley, *Poems* (New York: Funk and Wagnalls, 1887), p. 13.

73. Rose Cleveland to Holley, 23 January 1888, Flower Memorial Library.

74. Westbrook, *Acres of Flint,* p. 20.

75. John Greenleaf Whittier to Holley, 31 April 1888, Houghton Library, Harvard University.

76. Holley, *Poems*, pp. 37–39.

77. Holley, "Story," chapter 26.

78. Will Carleton to Holley, 3 July 1888, Flower Memorial Library.

5—BONNIE VIEW AND MAY

1. L. C. Hoxie, "Miss Holley's Garden Bright and Beautiful," *Watertown Daily Times,* 25 November 1938.

2. "Handyman-Secretary of Noted Writer, Marietta Holley, Tells How She Rose to Fame with Pen," *Watertown Daily Times,* no date.

3. Blyley, "Marietta Holley," p. 24.

4. Hart, *Popular Book,* p. 181.

5. Holley to John Greenleaf Whittier, 31 April 1888, Houghton Library, Harard University.

6. Holley, "Story," chapter 27; *Jefferson County Journal,* 20 November 1888.

7. *Jefferson County Journal,* 15 September 1891.

8. "Handyman-Secretary"; and Blyley, "Marietta Holley," p. 24.

9. E. B. Whitcomb, *Jefferson County Journal,* 15 May 1894. A few years later Holley had all the floor coverings removed and a parquet floor laid, but no reason for the change is evident (Blyley, "Marietta Holley," p. 24). Some of the photographs taken of the interiors during 1888 and early 1889 by Williams and Keller are in the collection at the Jefferson County Historical Society, Watertown, N.Y. Others are in the papers of Katherine Gillette Blyley.

10. Bode, *Anatomy,* p. 59.

11. *Jefferson County Journal,* 28 October 1890.

12. Ibid., 12 December 1893.

13. Ibid., 11 September and 18 September 1888.

14. Ibid., 15 January 1889.

15. Marietta Holley, *Josiah's Alarm and Abel Perry's Funeral* (Philadelphia: Lippincott, 1895), p. 29.

16. Papashvily, *Happy Endings, p. xv.*

17. *Jefferson County Journal,* 3 September 1889.

18. Frances Willard to Holley, 15 October 1889, Jefferson County Historical Society.

19. Mary B. Willard to Holley, 9 December 1889. Flower Memorial Library.

20. Wagnalls, "Glimpse," p. 61.

21. "An Interview With Miss Holley," *Rome Sentinel,* July 1903.

22. *Jefferson County Journal,* 25 February 1890.

23. Ibid., 22 April 1890.

24. Marietta Holley, *Samantha Among the Brethren* (New York: Funk and Wagnalls, 1890), p. xi.

25. Holley, "Story," chapter 27.

26. Kraditor, *Woman Suffrage,* pp. 76, 87.

27. *Jefferson County Journal,* 10 June 1890.

28. Wagnalls, "Glimpse."

29. *Jefferson County Journal,* 28 August 1894.

30. Frances Willard to Holley, 26 November 1890, Flower Memorial Library.

31. Holley, "How I Wrote My First Book," p. 404; and Blyley, "Marietta Holley," p. 28.

32. Bode, *Anatomy,* p. 184, and Wood, "The Scribbling Women and Fanny Fern: Why Women Wrote," *American Quarterly,* 23 (Spring 1971): 8.

33. Holley, "How I Wrote My First Book," p. 405.

34. *Jefferson County Journal,* 19 July 1892.

35. Ibid., 15 September 1891.

36. Holley, *Samantha on the Race Problem* (New York: Dodd, Mead, 1892), p. 159.

37. Ibid., p. 200.

38. *Jefferson County Journal,* 15 November 1893.

39. Holley, "Story," chapter 21.

40. *Jefferson County Journal,* 15 November 1893.

41. Ibid., 14 February 1893.

42. Ibid., 8 May 1893.

43. Ibid., 28 October 1890.

44. Holley, "Story," chapter 16.

45. Clara Barton to Holley, 29 May 1895, Library of Congress.

46. Holley, "Story" chapter 5.

47. Holley, *Samantha at the World's Fair* (New York: Funk and Wagnalls, 1893), p. 115.

48. Ibid., p. 685.

49. Clara Barton to Holley, 22 August 1893, Flower Memorial Library.

50. Holley, "Story," chapter 15.

51. "Judge Holley Dead," *Jefferson County Journal,* 26 September 1893.

52. Holley, "Story," chapter 16.

53. Ibid., chapter 15.

54. Holley, *Sweet Cicely,* p. vii.

55. Holley to Mrs. Eaton, 8 April 1904, State University College at Geneseo.

56. Holley, "Story," chapter 25.

57. Clara Barton to Holley, 18 December 1894, Library of Congress.

58. *Jefferson County Journal,* 3 May 1892 and 31 July 1894.

59. Ibid., 26 December 1893.

60. Inez McConnell, interview with author, 26 September 1980.

61. *Jefferson County Journal,* 20 February 1894.

62. "Marietta Holley At Home," *Jefferson County Journal,* 15 May 1894.

63. Ellen Moers, *Literary Women* (New York: Doubleday, 1976), p. 216.

64. *Jefferson County Journal,* 12 June 1894.

65. "Miss Holley's Home," *Jefferson County Journal,* 15 May 1894.

66. *Jefferson County Journal,* 7 August 1894 and 11 September 1894.

67. Holley, "Story," chapter 21.

68. *Jefferson County Journal,* 23 July 1895.

69. James Ford to Holley, undated, Flower Memorial Library.

70. Williams, *Clara Barton,* p. 273.

71. Clara Barton to Holley, September (no year), Letter Book 17, Library of Congress.

72. Holley to Clara Barton, 28 October 1895, Library of Congress.

73. Holley to Clara Barton, 6 January 1896, Library of Congress.

74. *Jefferson County Journal,* 28 January 1896.

75. Holley to Clara Barton, 6 January 1896, Library of Congress.

76. *Jefferson County Journal,* 28 June 1898.

77. Ibid., 20 October 1896; and Holley to Clara Barton, 12 February 1896, Library of Congress.

78. *Jefferson County Journal,* 15 September, 22 September, and 20 October 1896.

79. Ibid., 27 April 1897.

80. Wagnalls, "Glimpse."

81. Clara Barton to Holley, 15 May 1897, Letter Book 17, Library of Congress.

82. Holley to Clara Barton, 7 April 1897, Library of Congress.

83. Williams, *Clara Barton,* p. 353.

84. *Jefferson County Journal,* 11 February 1896, quoted from the Boston *Times.*

85. Holley, "Story," chapter 26.

86. Papashvily, *Happy Endings,* p. 148.

87. Holley, *Around the World With Josiah Allen's Wife* (New York: Dillingham, 1899), p. 142.

88. Holley to Clara Barton, 30 October 1897, Library of Congress.

89. Ibid.

90. *Jefferson County Journal,* 6 July 1897.

91. Ibid., 5 October 1897.

92. Ibid., 16 November 1897.

93. Holley to Clara Barton, 29 March 1898, Library of Congress.

94. *Jefferson County Journal,* 8 March 1898.

95. *Watertown Daily Times,* 11 July 1947.

96. Holley to Clara Barton, 31 May 1898, Library of Congress.

97. *Jefferson County Journal,* 6 December 1898; Holley, "Story," chapter 12; and Holley to Clara Barton, 19 December 1898, Library of Congress.

98. Holley to Clara Barton, 14 May 1897, Library of Congress.

99. *Jefferson County Journal,* 30 May 1899.

100. Will Carleton to Holley, 9 November 1899, Flower Memorial Library.

101. *Jefferson County Journal,* 25 July 1899.

102. Holley, "Story," chapter 14.

103. *Jefferson County Journal,* 5 September 1899.

104. Ibid., 9 October 1900.

6—BONNIE VIEW AND BEYOND

1. Holley, "Story," chapter 15.

2. Ibid., chapter 20.

3. Williams, *Clara Barton,* p. 425.

4. Holley, "Story," chapter 15.

5. Holley, "What Is Behind Ouija?", *World Magazine,* 27 June 1920, pp. 5, 13.

6. Holley, "Story," chapter 15.

7. Ibid.

8. Ibid., chapter 3.

9. Ibid., chapter 24.

10. Blyley, "Marietta Holley," p. 21.

11. Holley, "Story, chapter 24.

12. Ibid.

13. Williams, *Clara Barton,* p. 388.

14. *Jefferson County Journal,* 10 December 1907.

15. Ibid., 6 September and 11 October 1904.

16. Marietta Holley, *Samantha at the St. Louis Exposition* (New York: Dillingham, 1904), p. 23.

17. Ibid., p. 96.

18. *Jefferson County Journal,* 21 June 1904.

19. Clara Barton to Holley, undated, Flower Memorial Library.

20. *Jefferson County Journal,* 9 May 1905.

21. Ibid., 21 March 1905.

22. Marietta Holley, *Samantha Vs. Josiah: Being the Story of the Borrowed Automobile and What Came of It* (New York: Funk and Wagnalls, 1906), chapter 19.

23. *Jefferson County Journal,* 2 October 1894.

24. Holley, "Story," chapter 25.

25. *Jefferson County Journal,* 5 February 1907.

26. Ibid., 31 December 1907.

27. *Watertown Daily Times,* 6 August 1908.

28. Elizabeth Cady Stanton to Holley, 9 May (no year), Flower Memorial Library.

29. Marietta Holley, *Samantha on Children's Rights* (New York: Dillingham, 1909), p. 279.

30. Blyley, "Marietta Holley," p. 32.

31. Gladys Barnes, interview with author, 26 September 1980.

32. Bernice Lord to author, 15 November 1981.

33. Inez McConnell, interview with author, 26 September 1980.

34. Blyley, "Marietta Holley," p. 26.

35. Juanita Shutts Jones, interview with author, 17 October 1981.

36. Roy Franklin Pierce to author, 25 July 1981.

37. Jones, interview.

38. Barnes, interview.

39. *Jefferson County Journal,* 6 October 1909 and 23 February 1910.

40. Ibid., 14 February 1912.

41. Marietta Holley, *Betsey Bobbet: A Drama* (Adams, N.Y.: W. J. Allen, 1880).

42. Clara Barton to Holley, 1 May 1912, Flower Memorial Library.

43. Holley, "Story," chapter 12.

44. Ibid., chapter 26.

45. *Jefferson County Journal,* 8 July 1914.

46. Ibid., 5 December 1914.

47. Blair, *Horse Sense,* pp. 308–9.

48. Holley, "How I Wrote My First Book," p. 404.

49. Holley, "Story," chapter 4.

50. Holley to John B. Johnson, April 1922, Johnson, scrapbooks, vol. 22, *Watertown Daily Times.*

51. Ima Honaker Herron, *The Small Town in American Literature* (Durham, N.C.: Duke University Press, 1939), p. 334.

52. *Jefferson County Journal,* 6 January 1915.

53. Ibid., 9 February 1916.

54. *Watertown Daily Times,* 15 November and 11 December 1916.

55. *Jefferson County Journal,* 21 March 1917.

56. Ibid., 8 August 1917 and 23 October 1918.

57. Ibid., 24 September 1919.

58. Ibid., 17 December 1919.

59. Johnson, scrapbooks, vol. 22.

60. "Miss Holley—An Autobiography," *Watertown Daily Times,* 4 February 1931.

61. *Watertown Daily Times,* 27 February 1923.

62. *Jefferson County Journal,* 1 August 1923; and Douglas, *Feminization,* pp. 208–9.

63. Holley to Johnson, 6 December 1923, Johnson, scrapbooks, vol. 22.

64. Holley to Johnson, Johnson, scrapbooks, vol. 22.

65. *Watertown Daily Times,* 4 February 1931.

66. What remains of this manuscript is in the Rare Book Room, Meine Collection, University of Illinois at Urbana-Champaign.

67. Douglas, *Feminization,* p. 195.

68. *Watertown Daily Times,* 4 February 1931.

69. *Jefferson County Journal,* 15 July 1925.

70. Copeland, "More Memories."

71. Blyley, "Marietta Holley," p. 35.

72. *Watertown Daily Times,* 1 March 1926.

73. Blyley, "Marietta Holley," p. 35.

74. Copeland, "More Memories."

75. *Watertown Daily Times,* 1 March 1926.

EPILOGUE

1. *Watertown Daily Times,* 2 March 1926.

2. Copeland, "Memories of Marietta Holley."

3. *Watertown Daily Times,* 5 May 1926.

4. Blyley, "Marietta Holley," p. 36. Holley's writing table, with its spindle rim intact, is now at the Jefferson County Historical Society in Watertown, N.Y.

5. Ibid. Holley's will is filed with the county clerk, Watertown, N.Y.

6. Ibid., p. 16. This seems to be the badly damaged copy that is at the University of Illinois, which includes Holley's own introduction rather than the one that Johnson wrote. The whereabouts of the original manuscript sent to Johnson is unknown.

7. *Watertown Daily Times,* 9 July 1943.

8. "Handyman-Secretary."

9. *Watertown Daily Times,* 16 March 1926, and Blyley, "Marietta Holley," p. 36.

10. *Watertown Daily Times,* 20 August 1938 and 13 July 1947.

SOURCES

Baym, Nina. *Women's Fiction: A Guide to Novels by and about Women in America, 1820–1870.* Ithaca: Cornell University Press, 1978.

Blair, Walter. *Native American Humor 1800–1900.* New York: American Book, 1937.

———. *Horse Sense in American Humor.* Chicago: University of Chicago Press, 1942.

Blyley, Katherine Gillette. "Marietta Holley." Ph.D. diss. University of Pittsburgh, 1936.

Bode, Carl. *Anatomy of American Popular Culture.* Berkeley: University of California Press, 1959.

Brooks, Van Wyk. *The Flowering of New England 1815–1865.* New York: E. P. Dutton, 1936.

———. *New England: Indian Summer 1865–1915.* New York: E. P. Dutton, 1940.

Brown, Herbert Ross. *The Sentimental Novel in America.* Durham, N.C.: Duke University Press, 1942.

Bruère, Mrs. Martha. *Laughing Their Way: Women's Humor in America.* New York: Macmillan, 1934.

Butler, Ellis P. "Marietta Holley." *Mark Twain Quarterly* (Fall 1937): 13.

Cooles, Foster. "A Visit to Josiah Allen's Wife." *New York Mail and Express,* 27 February 1892.

Cott, Nancy F. *The Bonds of Womanhood: "Woman's Sphere" in New England 1780–1835.* New Haven: Yale University Press, 1977.

Cross, Whitney R. *The Burned-Over District: A Social and Intellectual History of Enthusiastic Religion in Western New York, 1800–1850.* New York: Harper and Row, 1965.

Curry, Jane Anne. "Women as Subjects and Writers of Nineteenth Century American Humor." Ph.D. diss. University of Michigan, 1975.

Douglas, Ann. *The Feminization of American Culture.* New York: Knopf, 1977.

Durant, S. W., and H. B. Pierce. *History of Jefferson County, New York.* Philadelphia: L. H. Everts, 1878.

Ehrenreich, Barbara, and Deirdre English. *Complaints and Disorders: The Sexual Politics of Sickness.* Old Westbury, N.Y.: The Feminist Press, 1973.

Ferguson, DeLancey. *Mark Twain: Man and Legend.* New York: Bobbs-Merrill, 1943.

Flexner, Eleanor. *Century of Struggle: The Woman's Rights Movement in the United States,* rev. ed. Cambridge, Ma.: Harvard University Press, 1975.

Florin, Lambert. *Ghost Towns of the West.* New York: Promontory Press, 1970, pp. 445–446.

Gilbert, Sandra M., and Susan Gubar. *The Mad Woman in the Attic: The Woman Writer and the Nineteenth-Century Literary Imagination.* New Haven: Yale University Press, 1979.

Graulich, Melody. "'Wimmen is my theme, and also Josiah': The Forgotten Humor of Marietta Holley." *American Transcendental Quarterly: A Journal of New England Writers* (Summer/Fall 1980): 187–97.

Haddock, John A. *The Growth of A Century; As Illustrated in the History of Jefferson County, New York from 1793–1894.* Albany: Weed-Parsons, 1895.

Hart, James D. *The Popular Book.* New York: Oxford University Press, 1950.

Hartman, Mary, and Lois Banner, eds. *Clio's Consciousness Raised.* New York: Harper and Row, 1974.

Herron, Ima Honaker. *The Small Town in American Literature.* Durham, N.C.: Duke University Press, 1939.

Holley, Marietta (Josiah Allen's Wife). *My Opinions and Betsey Bobbet's.* Hartford, Ct.: American Publishing, 1873.

———. *Josiah Allen's Wife as a P.A. and P.I.: Samantha at the Centennial.* Hartford, Ct.: American Publishing, 1877.

———. *Betsey Bobbet: A Drama.* Adams, N.Y.: W. J. Allen, 1880.

———. *The Lament of the Mormon Wife.* Hartford, Ct.: American Publishing, 1880.

———. *My Wayward Pardner; or, My Trials with Josiah, America, the Widow Bump, and Etcetery.* Hartford, Ct.: American Publishing, 1880.

———. *Miss Richard's Boy and Other Stories.* Hartford, Ct.: American Publishing, 1883.

———. *Sweet Cicely: Josiah Allen as a Politician*. New York: Funk and Wagnalls, 1885.

———. *Miss Jones' Quilting and Other Stories*. New York: J. S. Ogilvie, 1887.

———. *Poems*. New York: Funk and Wagnalls, 1887.

———. *Samantha at Saratoga or Flirtin' with Fashion*. Philadelphia: Hubbard Brothers, 1887.

———. *Samantha Among the Brethren*. New York: Funk and Wagnalls, 1890.

———. *Samantha on the Race Problem*. New York: Dodd, Mead, 1892; republished 1898 as *Samantha Among the Colored Folks*.

———. *Tirzah Ann's Summer Trip and Other Sketches*. New York: F. M. Lupton, 1892.

———. *Samantha at the World's Fair*. New York: Funk and Wagnalls, 1893.

———. *Widder Doodle's Love Affair and Other Stories*. New York: F. M. Lupton, 1893.

———. *Josiah's Alarm and Abel Perry's Funeral*. Philadelphia: Lippincott, 1895.

———. *Samantha in Europe*. New York: Funk and Wagnalls, 1895.

———. *Samantha at the St. Louis Exposition*. New York: G. W. Dillingham, 1904.

———. *Around the World With Josiah Allen's Wife*. New York: G. W. Dillingham, 1905.

———. *Samantha Vs. Josiah: Being the Story of the Borrowed Automobile and What Became of It*. New York: Funk and Wagnalls, 1906.

———. *Samantha on Children's Rights*. New York: G. W. Dillingham, 1909.

———. *Josiah's Secret*. Watertown, N.Y.: Hungerford-Holbrook, 1910.

———. "How I Wrote My First Books." *Harper's Bazaar* (September 1911).

———. *Samantha at Coney Island and a Thousand Other Islands*. New York: Christian Herald, 1911.

———. *Samantha on the Woman Question*. New York: Fleming H. Revell, 1913.

———. *Josiah Allen on the Woman Question*. New York: Fleming H. Revell, 1914.

———. "What Is Behind Ouija?" *The World Magazine* (27 June 1920): 5, 13.

———. "The Story of My Life," published serially. *Watertown Daily Times*, Watertown, N.Y., 5 February to 9 April 1931.

Hough, Franklin B. *A History of Jefferson County in the State of New York from the Earliest Period to the Present Time*. Watertown, N.Y.: Sterling and Riddell, 1854.

Johnson, Allen, ed. *Dictionary of American Biography*. New York: Scribner's, 1929.

Judson, Mrs. Russell. "First Area College Left Mark On Village." *Chatham Courier Supplement,* 19 October 1972, p. 6.

Kraditor, Aileen S. *The Ideas of the Woman Suffrage Movement, 1890–1920.* New York: Columbia University Press, 1965.

Landon, Harry F. *The North Country: A History Embracing Jefferson, St. Lawrence, Oswego, Lewis and Franklin Counties.* Indianapolis: Historical Publishing, 1931.

Madison, Charles A. *Book Publishing in America.* New York: McGraw-Hill, 1966.

Moers, Ellen. *Literary Women.* New York: Doubleday, 1976.

Moore, R. Lawrence. "Spiritualism and Science: Reflections on the First Decade of the Spirit Rappings." *American Quarterly* 29 (1972): 474–580.

———. "Spiritualist Medium: A Study of Female Professionals in Victorian America." *American Quarterly* 27 (1975): 200–21.

Morris, Linda Ann Finton. "Women Vernacular Humorists in Nineteenth Century America: Ann Stephens, Frances Whitcher, and Marietta Holley." Ph.D. dissertation, University of California, Berkeley, 1978.

Mott, Frank Luther. *History of American Magazines, 1865–1885.* Cambridge, Ma.: Harvard University Press, 1938.

———. *Golden Multitudes: The Story of Best Sellers in the United States.* New York: Macmillan, 1947.

———. *History of American Magazines, 1885–1905.* Cambridge, Ma.: Harvard University Press, 1957.

National Cyclopedia of American Biography. Clifton, N.J.: James T. White, 1979.

Nesbitt, Rosemary. *The Great Rope.* Oswego, N.Y.: Mathom, 1980.

Oakes, R. A. *Genealogical and Family History of Jefferson County, New York.* New York: Lewis, 1905.

O'Donnell, Thomas F. "The Regional Fiction of Upstate New York." Ph.D. dissertation, Syracuse University, 1957.

Papashvily, Helen Waite. *All The Happy Endings.* New York: Harpers, 1956.

Parker, Gail, ed. *The Ovenbirds: American Women on Womanhood 1820–1920.* New York: Anchor Books, 1972.

Pattee, F. L. *The Feminine Fifties.* New York: Appleton, 1942.

Rifkind, Carole. *A Field Guide to American Architecture.* New York: New American Library, 1980, Part I, pp. 61–97.

Ross, Ishbel. *Angel of the Battlefield: The Life of Clara Barton.* New York: Harper and Brothers, 1956.

Rourke, Constance. *American Humor: A Study of the National Character.* New York: Harcourt, Brace, 1931.

Spacks, Patricia Meyer. *The Female Imagination.* New York: Knopf, 1975.

Tandy, Jennette. *Crackerbox Philosophers in American Humor and Satire.* Port Washington, N.Y.: Kennikat Press, 1925.

Todd, Mabel Loomis, ed. *Letters of Emily Dickinson.* New York: Harper and Brothers, 1931.

Wagnalls, Mabel. "A Glimpse of Marietta Holley." *Ladies Home Journal* (November 1903): 61.

Watertown Daily Times, Watertown, N.Y.:

Copeland, Ella Page. "Home Memories of Marietta Holley and Her Family." 23 November 1934.

———. "More Memories of Marietta Holley and Her Family," 28 December 1934.

———. "Memories of Marietta Holley By One Who Knew Her Well," 10 October 1936.

Enos, Barton M. "Conversion of Josiah Allen's Wife" (no date).

Hoxie, L. C. "Miss Holley's Garden Bright and Beautiful," 25 November 1938.

Lane, David F. "Marietta Holley's Home Once Bright With Flowers," 8 November 1938.

"Josiah Allen's Wife At North Country Home," 10 July (no year).

"An Interview With Miss Holley," June 1903 (incomplete date).

"Handyman-Secretary of Noted Writer, Marietta Holley, Tells How She Rose to Fame With Pen" (no date).

"Poor Opinion of Movie Producers," 11 December 1916, p. 2.

"Betsey Bobbet May Be Filmed," 16 December 1921.

"Marietta Holley," 2 March 1926.

"Writer Leaves Her Home to Salvation Army," 19 March 1926.

"Burial of Miss Holley," 5 May 1926, p. 16.

"Marietta Holley Place Redeemed," 20 August 1938.

"Miss Holley's Garden and Beautiful Home," 25 November 1938.

"Romance of Marietta Holley Is Revealed," 9 July 1943, p. 10.

"Two of Marietta Holley's Manuscripts Are Found," 31 March 1945.

"Dedicating Bonnie View," 14 July 1947.

Welter, Barbara. *Dimity Convictions.* Athens, Oh.: Ohio University Press, 1976.

Westbrook, Perry D. *Acres of Flint: Sarah Orne Jewett and Her Contemporaries,* rev. ed. Metuchen, New Jersey: Scarecrow Press, 1981.

Williams, Blanche Colton. *Clara Barton, Daughter of Destiny.* New York: Lippincott, 1941.

Williams, Patricia. "The Crackerbox Philosopher As Feminist: The Novels of Marietta Holley." *American Humor: An Interdisciplinary Newsletter* 7, no. 1 (1980): 16–21.

Williamson, Mary Celeste. "Marietta Holley's Samantha." M.A. thesis, Catholic University of America, 1946.

Wilson, Edmund. *Upstate: Records and Recollections of Northern New York.* New York: Farrar, Straus and Giroux, 1971.

Wood, Ann Douglas. "The Scribbling Women and Fanny Fern: Why Women Wrote." *American Quarterly* 23 (Spring 1971): 3–24.

———. "The Literature of Impoverishment: The Women Local Colorists in America 1865–1914." *Women's Studies* 1, no. 1 (1972): 3–45.

INDEX